With a Machine Gun to Cambrai

GEORGE COPPARD

PAPERMAC

First published in hardback 1980 by the Imperial War Museum

First published in paperback 1986 by
PAPERMAC
a division of Macmillan Publishers Limited
4 Little Essex Street London WC2R 3LF
and Basingstoke

Associated companies in Auckland, Delhi, Dublin, Gaborone, Hamburg,
Harare, Hong Kong, Johannesburg, Kuala Lumpur, Lagos, Manzini,
Melbourne, Mexico City, Nairobi, New York, Singapore and Tokyo

British Library Cataloguing in Publication Data
Coppard, George
    With a machine gun to Cambrai.
    1. World War, 1914—1918—Campaigns   2. World
    War, 1914—1918—Personal narratives, British
    I. Title
    940.4'81'41   D546

ISBN 0-333-41687-2

Designed by Phil Kay

Filmset by BAS Printers Limited, Over Wallop, Hampshire
Printed in Hong Kong

With a Machine Gun to Cambrai

Vickers ·303 Machine Gun

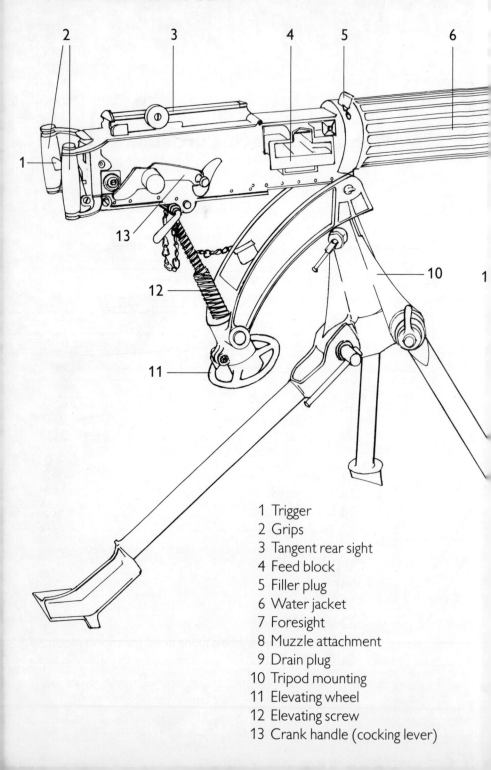

1 Trigger
2 Grips
3 Tangent rear sight
4 Feed block
5 Filler plug
6 Water jacket
7 Foresight
8 Muzzle attachment
9 Drain plug
10 Tripod mounting
11 Elevating wheel
12 Elevating screw
13 Crank handle (cocking lever)

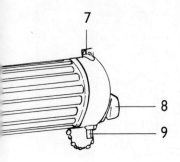

7

8

9

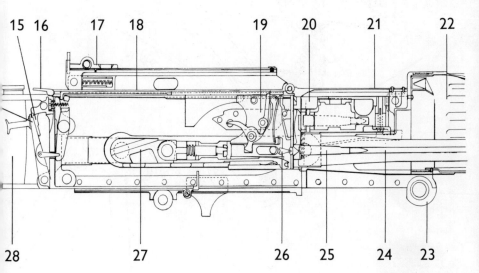

15 16   17   18   19   20   21   22

28   27   26   25   24   23

14 Trigger
15 Safety catch
16 Rear cover catch
17 Tangent rear sight
18 Rear cover (giving access to firing mechanism)
19 Lock frame
20 Feed block
21 Front cover (giving access to feed block)
22 Water jacket
23 Trunnion block (main fixing point for tripod mount)
24 Barrel
25 Chamber
26 Firing pin
27 Crank
28 Grip

Foreword

The Imperial War Museum, founded in 1917 and established by Act of Parliament in 1920, is now concerned with all aspects of the two world wars and other war-like activities in which Britain and the Commonwealth have been involved since 1914. Its object is to collect, preserve and display the greatest attainable range of objects, records and impressions which reflect the numerous facets of this vast and influential subject.

Of impressions, it may be that those of the eye-witness artist and author have the capacity to create the most immediate and the most moving appeal. It may be too that in these media, those appeals will reveal artistic and literary dividends of the highest order. The great art collection of the Imperial War Museum is evidence of the former possibility and one cannot read many pages of *With a Machine Gun to Cambrai* before recognising it as evidence of the latter possibility.

Hearing that the Museum was seeking to increase its collection of literary impressions, Mr Coppard sent me his manuscript, which he had composed on the basis of diaries he kept during the war. He kindly offered what he described as a 'plain soldier's tale' for the archives of the Imperial War Museum.

Naturally, we decided to publish the tale, for it is the product of a viewpoint enriched by a power of spontaneity which gives it a unique place in the literature of the First World War.

Noble Frankland, Director
Imperial War Museum

Preface

Of the scores of military reminiscences of the First World War, almost all are the work of officers or of men, who, though serving in the ranks, by education and upbringing belonged to the officer class. Some of these accounts, such as *Goodbye to All That* and *Undertones of War*, have become classics. But though the officer, particularly the junior infantry officer, had unique opportunities to observe and comment on the war, his was a special kind of experience. He was expected to set an example to his men and was thus more likely to get killed or wounded, but he enjoyed privileges which alleviated the hardships of life at the front. He was not constantly badgered and sworn at by sergeant-majors, and he escaped the physical drudgery which fell to those at the bottom of the military hierarchy. As Frank Richards remarked in *Old Soldiers Never Die* (the only narrative of the First World War to have been written by a regular private soldier) the war as seen from the point of view of those in the ranks was a 'different war'.

With a Machine Gun to Cambrai is about this other war. Mr Coppard, who describes himself as a 'common private of the uneducated classes', went to France as a very young volunteer and served as a machine gunner until 1917, when he was badly wounded. His book is not only an extremely lively and vivid account of his experiences on the Western Front but is also a social document of considerable importance. Mr Coppard is a sympathetic and sensitive observer, and some of his writing—for example, his description of the battlefield after the first day of the Somme—has a real emotional intensity. One feels that in his views on the war and on the manner in which it was waged Mr Coppard speaks for a whole generation of civilian Tommies.

What emerges most strikingly from his book is the helplessness of the private soldier in the face of a military system which demanded of him total and unquestioning obedience to the orders of his superiors, and which enforced those orders by severe penalties. If he was unpunctual, drunk, insolent, untidy or neglectful, he was liable to penalties ranging from fatigues to Field Punishment Number One, which involved his exposure for an hour or two each day with his hands tied to a waggon wheel. For serious offences, such as cowardice or desertion, the penalty was death. Although many of the death sentences passed by British courts martial were commuted to terms of imprisonment, on average one soldier was shot by a firing squad every week of the war. Yet, in the final analysis, it was not the threat of punishment which kept the British army in the field, nor was it patriotism, which seldom survived the first tour of duty in the trenches. The war was the supreme test of an individual's physical and mental stamina, and there were few who failed to respond to its challenge. Men endured the horrors and privations of trench warfare because their self-respect and their sense of duty would not allow them to give in. As Mr Coppard points out, this was particularly the case with the volunteer.

A certain amount of editing has been necessary, but care has been taken to preserve the flavour of the original text. The alterations have been approved by the author, who has helped in selecting the illustrations.

Christopher Dowling
Keeper of Education and Publications
Imperial War Museum

Preface to the hardback edition

When the original paperback edition of *With a Machine Gun to Cambrai* was published by HMSO for the Trustees of the Imperial War Museum in 1968 it was greeted with enthusiasm both by veterans of the First World War and by much younger readers. This hardback edition, which appears under the Museum's own imprint, has been produced in the belief that a work which has established itself as a classic of its kind should be available in a more permanent form. The text has been thoroughly revised and a certain amount of new material incorporated. In addition there is an epilogue, in which the author gives a moving account of his return to the battlefields of his youth, and a selection of the many letters which he received from old soldiers and their relatives.

Contents

List of illustrations

Introduction

For many years I have considered writing about my experiences in the 1914–1918 war, but although the passing years became decades and the succeeding decades totted up to half a century, a busy working life prevented me from getting down to it. During all that time I knew I possessed three battered notebooks I had carried in France, in which was recorded a good deal of what happened to me. With the coming of retirement, out came the notebooks. Reading the boyish scribble provided the key to unlock a store of memories, and I found no difficulty in reliving the excitement, drama and fears that I and my comrades shared so long ago.

My experiences in the 1939–1945 war, when I was seconded to the War Office as a special security officer and attached to the British and Allied Special Services, were fascinating, to say the least. But as a personal contribution to the war effort it was puny indeed when compared with the nerve-racking life I led as a boy in the trenches.

In the account which follows I have endeavoured to describe what happened to me, from the day I volunteered to the day I was demobbed, covering a period of four and a half years as an infantryman and machine gunner in the Queen's Royal West Surrey Regiment and the Machine Gun Corps.

I am grateful to my dear aunt, Mrs Emily Chester, who persuaded me to keep a diary of my doings in the Great War, without which I could never have written this narrative. This book is dedicated to my wife, Neilena, and our two daughters, Audrey and Sheila.

George Coppard
Tenterden, 1968

The author (seated) on convalescent leave, March 1918, with Sergeant E Walton, a relative.   *Imperial War Museum Q71266*

1 I join the Queen's, 2nd of Foot

Glossing over my childhood, I merely state that in 1914 I was just an ordinary boy of elementary education and slender prospects. Rumours of war broke out and I began to be interested in the Territorials tramping the streets in their big strong boots. Although I seldom saw a newspaper, I knew about the assassination of Archduke Ferdinand at Sarajevo. News placards screamed out at every street corner and military bands blared out their martial music in the main streets of Croydon. This was too much for me to resist, and as if drawn by a magnet I knew I had to enlist straight away.

I had no fixed ideas of what branch of the army I wanted to join and considered I would be lucky if I was accepted at all. Although weighing over ten stone I was very much a boy in heart and mind. Towards the end of August I presented myself to the recruiting sergeant at Mitcham Road Barracks, Croydon. There was a steady stream of men, mostly working types, queuing up to enlist. The sergeant asked me my age, and when told replied, 'Clear off son. Come back tomorrow and see if you're nineteen, eh?' So I turned up again the next day and gave my age as nineteen. I attested in a batch of a dozen others and, holding up my right hand, swore to fight for King and Country. The sergeant winked as he gave me the King's shilling, plus one shilling and ninepence ration money for that day. I believe he also got a shilling for each man he secured as a recruit.

I see from my discharge papers that I enlisted on 27 August 1914. As I was born on 26 January 1898, it follows that I was sixteen years and seven months old. The Battle of Mons had just been fought, and what was left of the Old Contemptibles was now engaged in the famous retreat. I knew nothing about all this. Like a log flung into a giant river, I had only just started to move. Later on I was to be pushed from behind, relentlessly, without any chance of escape.

Late that afternoon, looking definitely crummy and un-washed, our motley crowd of recruits shuffled up to East Croydon station and took a train for Guildford, final destination Stoughton Barracks. I gathered that this was the headquarters of the Royal West Surrey Regiment, otherwise known as The Queen's, 2nd of Foot. The regiment was formed in honour of

Queen Catherine of Braganza, the Portuguese wife of King Charles II. The regimental badge was a lamb, which somehow seemed too mild to be a symbol for fighting men. As a young rookie expecting fireworks, something fiercer-looking would have suited me better. Old soldiers usually referred to us as the 'Mutton Lancers'.

On our arrival at Stoughton there was a rush to the canteen to spend what was left of the ration money. A roll call took place, and there were two or three absentees. I never did learn what happened. Could it be that they attested merely to get two shillings and ninepence?

Reveille was at 5.30 am next morning and, after a night on the floor with half a blanket, I didn't feel too good. Word flashed round that 'gunfire' (tea) was available at the cookhouse. A scramble followed, but there were few mugs to drink from. I drank mine from a soup plate, not an easy task at the first attempt. After a day or two of this kind of thing, I realised that I had left the simple decencies of the table at home. One had to hog it or else run the risk of not getting anything at all. I learnt this lesson quicker than anything else.

Looking round at my new companions I could see that several were near-tramps. One wore a faded old morning coat and a well-bashed bowler. With his big draggled moustache he looked a perfect carbon copy of 'Old Bill' of the 'Better Hole' fame. We called him 'Uncle' and he seemed to relish the title. For about a week we were chased about on elementary drill and fatigues, with PT thrown in, and then we moved to Purfleet in Essex. Our first job was pitching a lot of bell-tents under the supervision of a batch of NCOs, some of whom were regular army and others re-enlisted men. They proceeded to treat us in the traditional manner as if we were a music-hall joke. The tent-pitching job gave them the opportunity to administer a sort of baptism of fire, and by the time the tents were up I was almost wishing I had never enlisted.

As tents were in short supply, the maximum number of recruits were allotted to each one. If I remember correctly the figure was twenty-two. Not having been in a tent before, I had no idea that it had twenty-two separate pieces of canvas sewn together to form the roof. The flap was the point of entry and, with twenty-two men stampeding to get in, somebody had to get the flap division as his portion of territory. I got it. This meant that I couldn't lie down at night until everyone was in the tent. When the tent was full, forty-four feet arranged in tangled layers converged in the general direction of the centre pole.

Nights were a nightmare to me and I dreaded them. Outside the tent flap within a yard of my head stood a urinal tub. Throughout the night boozy types would stagger and lunge towards the flap in order to urinate. I got showered every time and, worst of all, it became a joke. At last revulsion overcame me, and one night I suddenly went berserk and lashed out violently at someone. There followed a riotous eruption and the tent collapsed. Luckily more tents became available, and from then on I managed to avoid the entry flap.

The camp was near Purfleet rifle ranges, and a battalion of the Guards were our neighbours under canvas. They were engaged in a full musketry course and the rattle of fire with ball ammunition went on all day long. The concentrated noise of '15 rounds rapid fire' thrilled me, never having heard anything more deadly than a 'Lewes Rouser'[1] on bonfire nights.

During this time we recruits were still in civvies. We looked a most untidy lot and the conditions under which we lived didn't help matters. I was wearing a straw boater when I enlisted, but it disappeared before I left Stoughton. Being hatless was tantamount to a crime, and drew scorn and dire threats from every NCO I came in contact with. I was forced to pay two shillings and sixpence per week for the loan of a begrimed khaki cap from the company cook, a cunning old South African veteran.

As if to complete the picture of utter ineptitude, dummy rifles were issued to us. However, the wheels of war industry were gathering speed, and soon issues of uniforms and equipment were made almost daily. By the end of September most of us had uniforms, either khaki or navy blue. I was bucked at getting khaki, which meant that I could give the cook his hat and escape his clutches.

Meals were cooked in field-kitchens and eaten in marquees, two sittings each meal. The orderly officer, accompanied by the

[1] A home-made rocket used in Lewes, Sussex, on Guy Fawkes night around the turn of the century. It exploded with a big bang and was dangerous if mishandled. Domestic animals were terrified by the noise it made.

orderly sergeant, would attend each meal and perform the usual ritual. The sergeant would breathe fire, smack his cane on a table and yell out, 'Orderly officer! Any complaints?' Now and then a bold type would do an Oliver Twist and wangle an extra spoonful of bodge. Although I was always hungry I never had enough nerve to complain. Any money I had was invariably spent on buns, pies and other odds and ends in the canteen.

It was rumoured that the gunfire was laced with jalap, but I was never able to find out the truth of this. It was probably an old soldier's yarn calculated to disturb the minds of rookies like me. PT followed gunfire at 6 am, a mad half-hour of press-ups and what not. The big thing was musketry, and there is no doubt we were trained to be good riflemen. The Guards battalion finished their course and it was our turn to go on the range.

A day or two before the Guards left the camp I heard a loud cheer in our lines, and there, passing within a foot of me, was the Prince of Wales (later King Edward VIII) in the uniform of a second lieutenant. His slim stooping figure rather surprised me. He looked very young and was carrying a paper bag, which I felt pretty sure contained cakes.

Our first shooting practice was on the miniature range with Lee Enfield .22 bore rifles. Then came the real stuff with .303 ammunition. I was a bit nervy at the prospect and wondered about the kick, but it was not so forceful as I expected. During the course I took my turn at the butts, an alarming experience at first. Quite often the bullets would strike something hard and make a fearsome howl. Once, a bullet ended its flight spinning like a top on the concrete floor beside me. Duly warned of the danger, I kept well back under the canopy during the firing. The range was close to the Thames, where the hooting of ships and river craft went on day and night.

By the end of October, with the steady arrival of recruits, the battalion strength was nearly completed. My regimental number was 701 and my official address was 13 Platoon, 'D' Company, 6th Battalion, The Queen's Royal West Surrey Regiment. We were part of the new army being formed throughout the country—Kitchener's Army. The CO's name was Lieutenant-Colonel Warden, a regular army officer. 'A' Company CO and second-in-command of the battalion was Major Watson, also a regular. I regret that I cannot remember for certain the name of 'B' Company's CO but I think it was Captain Butler. Captain Rolls was CO of 'C' Company, and a regular army officer. My own CO was Captain Hull, a regular too. It is a pity that I cannot supply the initials of these gentlemen.

They were a most immaculate and elegant set, right out of the world of my youthful experience. One of them wore a monocle occasionally, which to my mind was a staggering addition to an already god-like appearance. A curious item of their dress was the stiff white collar worn with their khaki uniforms. Junior officers wore khaki collars, but later on senior officers followed suit in favour of khaki neckwear. Maybe laundering difficulties had something to do with it.

At this time, indeed for many months to come, I was chiefly concerned with 13 Platoon, and then 'D' Company. My world never really extended beyond that bounded by company control. Company drill was a regular feature of our training but we seldom drilled as a battalion, and when we did the results were not very good. My platoon officer was Lieutenant Clarke. Somebody said that he was an Oxford don, but that meant little to me then. He was about thirty years old, and looked a distinguished and powerful man. He was sincere and kindly, with a cultured voice which I can hear in my memory to this day. From a distance I admired Captain Hull very much, but I used to wonder if he ever noticed me in the ranks at all. He was tall, slim and upright, with blond hair and a cropped moustache. Like all the company COs he had magnificent tan riding boots and jingling spurs. In my youthful opinion he was undoubtedly the handsomest and smartest soldier in the battalion.

We recruits were always in trouble with our uniforms, which were either too big or too small. No amount of alterations by the battalion tailor produced the desired results. There must have been some pretty skimpy inspections by the War Office to pass the misfits we had to put up with. The flawless appearance of the officers multiplied our inferiority complex no end. My particular weakness at first was putting on puttees—the khaki leg bandages used in the Indian Army—and many a choking-off I got because the windings bulged a bit.

Gradually I developed a streak of obstinacy, and would show my inward rebellion by a scowling countenance or baleful glare.

This behaviour was fatal and I had to pay for it. Once on line of march I glared round at the NCO in charge, an elderly re-enlisted man, when he bawled out my name for some misdemeanour or other. He gave me verbal hell, and when we dismissed he marched me off to the guardroom and charged me with dumb insolence. The next morning Captain Hull gave me four days' CB (confined to barracks) and a frigid lecture. From then on I learned to mask my feelings and acquired the art of blowing raspberries, which one of my companions was a past master at.

'Jankers' was the common name for CB. From the moment of sentence I became liable to the whims and dictates of the police sergeant. Starting at two or three minutes after reveille and other such awkward times, the bugler would blast out a call which, translated into words, went: 'You can be a defaulter as long as you like, as long as you answer your name.' With other defaulters I had to run at the double to the police tent, answer my name and get told off to my fatigue. The Lord help you if you were late. It was an offence to be late, and usually meant another dose of Jankers. Emptying the urinal tubs was always the first job; you could bank on it. Other fatigues, such as peeling spuds, washing thousands of plates and doing cookhouse chores, succeeded each other with monotonous regularity throughout the day. At night it would be washing up at the officers' mess, where a tasty morsel was sometimes proffered, or, if not, pilfered, from the left-overs. I like to think I enjoyed Jankers, for it gave me the excuse to grouse, a soldier's traditional privilege. In a sense it was an important part of my army training learning how to be fly and cunning. As the youngest in the battalion I had to accept the leg-pulls of the older men, and I've no doubt this did me a lot of good.

Petty gambling began to catch on, though Heaven knows there wasn't much money about. A private earned a bob a day—three shillings and sixpence a week if he made an allowance to a dependent. On pay nights, like a lamb to the slaughter, I allowed myself to be roped in for a plucking, hoping a miracle would happen and I'd clean up the lot. The favourite games were Brag, Pontoon, and Crown and Anchor. After an hour or so I'd be broke and become a hanger-on, a suppliant for small favours, earned by running messages for the rest of the 'school'. I'd stagger from the canteen with pints of beer and eats, and get my reward, a fag perhaps.

I must plead guilty here to a bit of unpremeditated chicanery. Paper money had just been issued for one pound and ten shillings, the design and size being very similar. One of the gambling kings handed me a ten-shilling note to buy him cigarettes. The canteen was packed, and in the noise and confusion I was given change of a pound. I shot out like a long-dog. Although my conscience troubled me I kept the excess cash just the same.

At weekends we were often given leave and free rail passes. Home to Croydon I'd go, taking full advantage of the free rides for servicemen in uniform on the London buses and trams. Towards the middle of November the battalion finished its musketry course. The weather grew cold and life under canvas lost all its glamour for me.

2 To winter quarters

On 20 November we left Purfleet for Sandling, Kent. Thick snow covered the ground. The wooden huts which were to be our winter quarters were barely finished and carpenters were working everywhere. The cold was intense, and chills and colds spread quickly. The medical officer was under some pressure with the growing sick parades. More for the experience than anything else, I tried my hand at going sick but got MD (medicine and duty) for my pains. This was a rude awakening for me. What was it the other sick-parade merchants had got that I hadn't got? Could they put on the agony better than I could, or was it that I was just bubbling over with good health?

The bad weather continued. Life in the huts was miserable, especially as we were plagued by kit inspections every week. Our kit had to be laid out to proper pattern and order: knife, fork, spoon, razor, comb, lather brush and so on. A good deal of pinching was going on and I found myself minus some articles. Deductions from my pay for the losses made me realise more than ever that I was in the army. The swiping of kit was a regular feature at Sandling, and the only thing I could do was a bit of counter-swiping.

During our stay in the huts a big fellow singled me out for bullying and foul abuse. I tried to keep out of his way, but there was no escaping the fact that I was his particular piece of meat. I got no comfort from the other chaps in the hut, for they sensed the possibility of fistic manoeuvres, an ever-welcome break in the monotonous routine of camp life. It boiled up one Sunday after church parade when I was sitting on a bench seat beside the bogey stove. In came the big fellow, who decided that I must be shifted to make room for him. He gave me a violent nudge along the seat, which deposited me on the floor. Immediately I got up he fetched me a nasty wallop beside the ear and challenged me to go outside. This could only mean a scrap, and before I had time to think it over I was unceremoniously bundled outside the hut by the boys. They made a ring, in the centre of which were the two of us, the big fellow and I, braces dangling, shirt sleeves rolled up. The Lord knows I was not a bit anxious to clash with this bloke, for to tell the truth I was in a state of funk. I can't even remember his name.

Just before I was prodded into action by the crowd around us I noticed that my antagonist was very flushed-looking. This I took to be an outward sign of his rage boiling up but, unknown to him or me, he was on the verge of an epileptic fit. When we met I struck out, and down he went kicking and foaming in fearful convulsions. He was carried into the hut and had to be held down on the bed. This was the first time I had witnessed such a seizure and it was an alarming experience. Eventually the MO arrived, and soon an ambulance carted the poor chap off to hospital. Maybe I did him a good turn, for within a month he was discharged as medically unfit. In the meantime I was in a state of remorse, waiting for the axe. To my amazement and relief the thing died down. From then on my stock definitely went up a little. Someone in the hut remarked, 'Blimey, what a wallop!'—a phrase that caught on for a while.

The continued severity of the weather and the unfinished condition of the huts precipitated a move; quite suddenly the battalion marched to Hythe and occupied billets on the sea front. Along with five other privates, I was billeted with Sergeant Morgan of 13 Platoon. He was a giant of a man, weighing eighteen stone, but not fat. In civvy life he was a police inspector in the Port of London Authority force and he wore South

African War medals. His growl was deep in his boots and he had a tiny spear-like moustache. I had a deep respect for him, for his great size awed me.

Our landlady, although very old, was a first-rate cook and did all our washing and mending. Having no visitors to attend to, she looked after us as if we were her own sons. I believe she received twenty-six shillings per week for the privates, which was good money then. Christmas Day in the billet was a day to be remembered, with lashings of good food and beer.

For the next two months the battalion, now almost at full strength, engaged in hard training, which included night operations, bayonet drill and firing on the local rifle range. Fixing bayonets was a tricky business. The sergeant instructor used to say, 'On the command "Fix", you don't fix, but on the command "Bayonets", you whips 'em out.' To the tune of 'D'ye ken John Peel', we sang the following verse:

> Now, dress by the right, boys, and get into line,
> First by numbers, and then judging the time,
> For you whips 'em out, and whops 'em on,
> And lets 'em bide awhile,
> That's the way you fix yer bayonets in the morning.

My seventeenth birthday occurred on 26 January 1915, while I was at Hythe.

3 Aldershot

We were starting to shape like real soldiers and I began to wonder when we would go overseas. At the end of February came another move, this time as part of our training. The battalion assembled and commenced the first stage of marching to Aldershot, roughly a hundred miles, in full kit, less ammunition. The march was done in easy stages and took nine days. At East Grinstead we marched past Sir Archibald Hunter, GOC Aldershot Command. The next day Lord Kitchener became the highlight on our journey. There was a good deal of wind-up before this event, and we were ordered to make a model salute and look straight into Kitchener's eyes. On the command 'Eyes right', I swung my head smartly and stared searchingly into the grey eyes. I was disappointed, for they were so heavily hooded. In his greatcoat Kitchener looked very big, but so baggy and grey—nothing like the dark handsome posters of him which were displayed all over the country. Still, the event was recognised as important to us at that time. We represented some of the earliest members of Kitchener's New Army of 70 divisions. The field-marshal lived long enough to know about the severe mauling our division, the 12th, got at Loos and the Hohenzollern Redoubt.

A little footsore, for army boots take a lot of working in, the battalion marched on to the great parade square at South Camp, Aldershot, the Mecca of the British Army. After inspection by the CO we dismissed and poured into Barossa Barracks. These consisted of a number of old red-brick blocks, barren and comfortless, or so they seemed after the Hythe billets. Red-capped military police were much in evidence, especially in the town. From the moment of our arrival we laboured under a much stiffer yoke of discipline than we had been accustomed to. Our CSM was named Annis, a re-enlisted man. He was very military-looking with his fierce black moustache and reminded me somewhat of the Kaiser himself. He drove his NCOs and they in turn drove us. Everything was done at the double from reveille to lights-out. It was all rather exciting, for although we didn't realise it we were gradually being transformed into efficient infantrymen.

A lot of time and not a little of our pay was spent on acquiring the maximum degree of spit and polish. To fail in this was as good as asking for permanent Jankers. The manufacturers of 'Soldier's Friend' and 'Blanco' reaped a rich harvest from the Aldershot Command.

The weeks flew by and then I was suddenly picked for a royal guard. King George V was coming to watch the manoeuvres of several battalions of the New Army which were now working up to fighting pitch. The guard consisted of Lieutenant Clarke of 13 Platoon, two sergeants, eighteen privates and a trumpeter. Two cooks were detailed to look after the grub side. For two weeks we drilled until we reached Guardsman-like efficiency, and I swatted up the typed instructions for the sentries to word perfection. His Majesty arrived and took up residence in the Royal Pavilion, which was guarded for one week by The Royal

Scots, 1st of Foot, the senior infantry regiment. Our guard detachment, representing the next most senior regiment, took over for the second week of His Majesty's stay.

A pal and I were posted on the main gate. Each of us had a sentry box and a strip of asphalt on which to pace up and down, and we could chat to each other across the road. The guardroom was fifty yards or so from the main gate. I had received instructions to turn out the guard whenever the King approached. Within an hour of our taking up our posts, a bowler-hatted detective tipped us off that the King and his party were leaving the pavilion. In the loudest voice I could command I bawled, 'Guard, turn out!' On the instant the guard rushed out of the guardroom and formed in line, the officer in front with drawn sword and the trumpeter at the ready. I glanced across to the royal mews and was amazed to see the King, dressed in khaki field-marshal's uniform, mount a splendid black charger. A pale blue plume was suspended underneath its head and bits of embroidered trappings ornamented the shining harness. The entire party, numbering some thirty riders, was headed by a civilian police sergeant. The officer gave the order, 'Guard, present arms!' As he swept his sword down towards the ground, the guard simultaneously smacked the magazines of their rifles with commendable precision and the trumpeter blew the royal salute. I was thrilled as the King passed by, acknowledging the salute of my pal and me at the gate, followed by the Prince of Wales, Lord Kitchener, Sir Archibald Hunter, Winston Churchill and a score of other high-ranking officials.

To keep us on our toes the lord-in-waiting for the day inspected the guard every morning. At night I frequently challenged shadowy figures who revealed themselves as detectives. Once or twice my itching trigger finger nearly got the better of me. Croaking frogs kicked up a row in the darkness, making things more spooky. One morning Queen Mary honoured us by visiting the guardroom. Accompanied by two ladies-in-waiting, she inspected our rations and appeared very interested. It was generally thought we were on officer's rations for we lived like fighting cocks that week.

A word about the canteen in South Camp. It was a large hall with a stage where low-brow variety turns did their stuff every night. At the other end, beer was sold in pint tin mugs (there were no half-pints) at tuppence a pint. The gravity was pretty good too, and a pint was as much as I could manage. There was a five-piece band and when the beer flowed the old-time songs got going. Men really did sing in that canteen. You could hear them a mile off. On pay nights Red Caps waited outside for closing time; it was an exciting spectacle watching the drunks trying to avoid arrest. There were few barrack rooms where gambling of some sort was not in full swing, even after lights-out. Blankets drawn closely together underneath a table screened the contestants as they played by candle-light. I remember an orderly sergeant whose job, among others, was to enforce lights-out in the barracks. When all was in darkness he'd dive under the blanketed table in our room, where a 'school' was always in session and the clink of money went on far into the night.

I became a card fiend for a while, but my luck was ruinous. Hunger made me give it up, as lack of money was depriving me of canteen suppers. I could get sausages and mash or liver and bacon for fivepence, and a chunk of bread for a halfpenny. Eating was my biggest worry at Aldershot for supper was not supplied as part of our rations. Occasionally word would drift round that there was soup in the cook-house. Only those with no cash took advantage of the offer, and I was generally among the poor and needy. The word calories as we know it today never existed in Aldershot. The Quartermaster-General never considered the needs of a growing body engaged on hard training, trench digging or route marching. The army clerk at his desk received the same amount of rations. Borrowing half-a-crown to buy extra grub became a habit with me, for by Monday or Tuesday I never had a penny left; and pay day was not until Friday.

There was a pub in the town called The Crimea, which in those days had a nasty reputation as a meeting place for prostitutes. Some of my pals frightened me with their talk of the loose women who haunted the place, and of such things as syphilis and gonorrhoea. I passed this pub one Saturday night when two women were flung out fighting. They continued the fight on the pavement and landed in the gutter tearing each other's hair out.

Time was now running out for the battalion. Night operations, mock battles with blank cartridges, route marches in all weathers—all played their part in putting the finishing touches to our fighting fitness. How fit we really were none of us knew. For my part, I knew that my rifle was my best friend, and I had a real affection for it. As for our CO, he might have been the Shah of Persia for all I knew of him. He had fought in the South African War and I trusted that he had the necessary experience to lead us to battle in the proper military way. We now had an adjutant, a tall handsome chap whose name, I think, was Captain Bassett. By this time the senior officers had horses, and when the battalion slogged it on route marches these gentlemen were comfortably seated.

I should say a few words about the machine gun section. Two Vickers machine guns were now allotted to the battalion. Reserve teams were required and I was picked out of the blue. This was a welcome surprise and I became a keen and willing learner. The Vickers .303 water-cooled gun was a wonderful weapon, and its successful use led to the eventual formation of the Machine Gun Corps, a formidable and highly-trained body of nearly 160,000 officers and men. Devotion to the gun became the most important thing in my life for the rest of my army career.

Rumours of our impending departure for overseas began to spread. A hair-shearing parade was ordered and every NCO and man had his hair shorn off close. I never noticed that the officers' hair was clipped with the same severity. The next thing to astonish us was an order abolishing the cleaning of buttons and other bright parts of our equipment. Every piece of brass had to be dulled like gun-metal, and bottles of acid were issued for the purpose. Whoops of joy swept through the ranks. Never was there such speed in putting an order into effect. Even the blades of our bayonets did not escape the tarnishing process, for nothing that might gleam or glint in the sunlight was exempt from the prohibition. Surely this was the most revolutionary order ever given in the British Army. The lads fairly howled with delight as 'Soldier's Friend' was flung away by the hundredweight. 'If that's how they bleedin' well want it, that's how they're bleedin' well going to get it,' remarked a wag.

I went down with an attack of tonsillitis and found myself in Connaught Hospital for a week. This was the first time I had ever been in a hospital as a patient. It was a new experience to be in bed in the day-time and it enabled me to indulge in a little quiet thinking without barrack-room interruptions or threats. I read grim reports in the newspapers of conditions in Gallipoli and France, and wondered to what front the battalion would be sent.

Shortly after my discharge from hospital, overseas leave started, and I went with the first batch. Some barrack-room lawyer told me that all entries on a soldier's crime sheet were expunged when he went overseas. On hearing this I was tempted to overstay my leave and, reckoning that there was

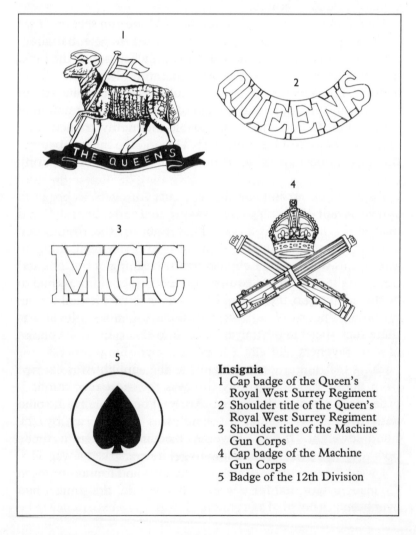

Insignia
1 Cap badge of the Queen's Royal West Surrey Regiment
2 Shoulder title of the Queen's Royal West Surrey Regiment
3 Shoulder title of the Machine Gun Corps
4 Cap badge of the Machine Gun Corps
5 Badge of the 12th Division

some doubt about my eventual survival, I took three extra days. It was a stupid thing to do, but somehow I owed it to myself to do something in defiance of authority. I avoided the Red Caps, but on my return I was clapped in the guardroom forthwith. However, I was considerably relieved when I learnt that the battalion had not sailed without me. My punishment from the CO was seven days' Jankers, plus a nasty dressing-down. Overstaying leave was worked by a lot of the lads, no doubt calculating that three extra days was well worth seven days' CB. The police sergeant had his work cut out, for there were more defaulters than work to keep them busy. Those with no work got pack drill.

Sergeant Morgan of 13 Platoon now left us, as he was too old for overseas service. His place was filled by Sergeant Fulbrook from the 2nd Battalion, The Queen's, another fine-looking soldier. Any drum major would have envied his proud strut. Very soon he became 'D' Company sergeant-major.

There was great activity in Aldershot and we soon heard that we were being sent to France as part of the 37th Infantry Brigade. The other three battalions were the 6th Battalion, Royal East Kents, commonly known as The Buffs, the 6th Battalion, Royal West Kents, and the 7th Battalion, Royal East Surreys. The brigade formed part of the 12th Division, the other two brigades being the 35th and the 36th. According to an old notebook I still have, a division consisted of headquarters, 3 infantry brigades, 3 Royal Field Artillery brigades, 1 howitzer brigade, 1 heavy battery and ammunition column, 3 field companies of Royal Engineers, 1 signal company of Royal Engineers, 1 cavalry squadron, 3 field ambulance units and 1 divisional train. The GOC of the 12th Division was Major-General F D V Wing, CB, CMG.

During the last few days before our departure for France my Uncle Alfred came to see me on his motor-bike and of course I had to have a ride on the thing, which was quite an event for a youngster in those days. I carried the memory of this with me to the trenches for reliving during the many lonely hours to come. My uncle and I were very close to each other, and he kept up a welcome correspondence throughout my sojourn in France. Later he became well known as A E Coppard, the short story writer.

Came 31 May 1915 and the battalion went on the binge, as it was our last night in Aldershot. The next day we left for Folkestone. A packet-boat called the *Invicta* sneaked out of the harbour at 9.45 pm with the battalion on board, destination Boulogne.

4 Overseas

So there I was, in France at last, with one of the first divisions of Kitchener's New Army. I was very excited at being on foreign soil for the first time. We marched through Boulogne and up the long drag to St Martin's camp. I remember a dreary wait for something to eat. On the way to the railway station next morning, French womenfolk crowded the streets to watch us, and a good deal of bantering went on as we passed. A few of the boys with a smattering of the lingo at their command tried out diabolical samples as greetings, such as, 'Vous jig-a-jig avec me tonight ma chérie?' The women took it all in good part, screaming with laughter. 'Tommee! Tommee!' they shouted as they tossed biscuits and chocolate to us.

At the station the train, composed of covered freight trucks each marked '40 Hommes 8 Chevaux', lay waiting. After we had been told off in batches of forty men there was a wild scramble to get on board, not an easy job with nearly three-quarters of a hundredweight of kit per man and forty rifles poking about. I sat on the side of the open doorway, legs dangling over the edge. The countryside looked beautiful and I felt as if I was taking part in a Sunday-school treat. The rail journey ended at St Omer, and a short march from there brought us to Eaure, where we were billeted in lofts and barns. The next day the march continued to a village near Hazebrouck, a distance of 24 kilometres. Quite a number of men succumbed to the sun's heat and got a lift on a transport limber.

The fall-out rule of ten minutes each hour of marching was maintained, but after three or four hours a fall-out became more like a collapse. Men literally crashed down with a great clatter of equipment and falling rifles. Once on the ground the technique was to slacken the belt, slide forward and use the pack as a pillow. Often a man would fall asleep and reel like a drunk when trying to stand up. If his feet were blistered and bleeding, he was in a sorry state. When the whistles blew and the cry, 'Fall in!' echoed down the long prostrate column, the moans and groans would start. Like a tortoise, my home was on my back. My pockets bulged with bits and pieces. It was not easy trying to grow to manhood loaded like a pack animal.

Junior officers had things a little easier for they marched in 'light order', or with a dummy pack with little or nothing in it and a cane under their arm. Any belongings of a weighty nature were packed in their valises by their batmen and put on transport. As if to remind us of the inferiority of our station, the colonel and company COs, looking soldierly and unfatigued, rode well-groomed horses. Looking at it today it seems a display of class privilege, but fifty years ago the Tommy accepted it as the natural order of things, for the changes enjoyed by the masses now were not even thought of.

The march continued towards the trenches and, after passing through Strazeele, the battalion entered the picturesque old town of Meteren, which was close to the Belgian frontier. The Germans had occupied the town some months before, and I was greatly stirred by a dramatic story of what had happened when they were driven out. An enemy machine gun had been mounted at the top of the church tower and a large party of our troops were caught by its fire. Heavy casualties were inflicted, and thirty graves bore evidence of this in the little cemetery near the church. Rough retaliation was quickly dealt to three German gunners. A British sergeant, armed with rifle and bayonet, crept up the spiral stairs of the church tower. Bayoneting two of the crew, he wrestled with and overpowered the third, flinging him from the top of the tower. This grim and heroic tale moved us all deeply. I wondered if I would be able to strike a blow at the enemy, or if I would get knocked out before getting a chance, like the chaps in the little cemetery nearby.

We had a pay parade while in the town: 5 francs per man. A franc was worth tenpence then, and ordinary wine cost half a franc a litre. I chummed up with a country lad named Marshall, who was fair-haired and a year older than I was. We usually shared a litre of *vin blanc*, which was more than enough to make us squiffy. Some of the houses displayed notices: 'Oeufs et pommes de terre frites, 50 centimes'. With a huge slice of

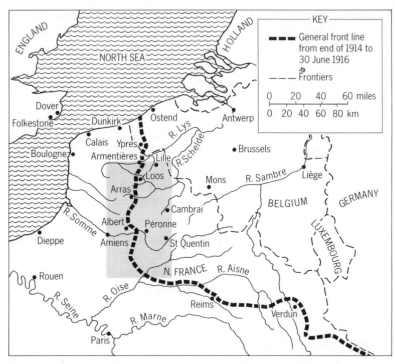

The Western Front, 1915 (shaded area shown in detail opposite).

country bread, plus a nip of cognac in the coffee, the total cost came to one franc. In the evenings we would stroll up a little street with terraced houses on both sides, and women sitting outside their doors making lace. Some of them were very old and were quaintly dressed in peasant costume. The lace took shape on cushions resting on their laps. With the aid of pins and dozens of spools of thread, which they deftly criss-crossed, the patterns developed. Each movement made a clicking sound, and in the quiet summer evening the whole street chattered with tiny clicks. The women laughed and joked as they worked and we joined in, though not understanding what they were talking about. They tried to sell us some lace but we were broke. Ypres was not far away, and now and then the sound of artillery rumbled towards us.

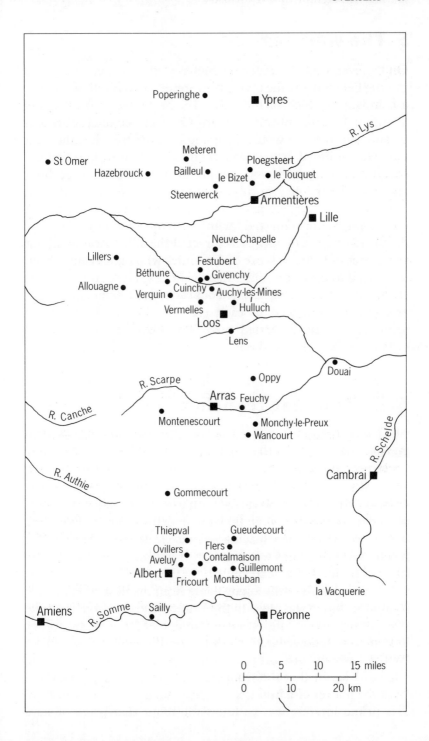

5 The warning

On the evening before leaving Meteren, the battalion marched to a big field outside the town. We formed up in a hollow square, a company on each of the sides. In the centre stood Colonel Warden, the adjutant and company COs. The colonel addressed us and said that we would be going into the trenches the next day. He reminded us that we were on a war footing and that the severest military laws would apply for any dereliction of duty, such as desertion, mutiny, leaving the trenches without permission, cowardice and sleeping while on sentry duty. A conviction by court martial for any such offence would carry the death sentence. The CO then directed the adjutant to read out the names of nearly a score of Tommies who had recently been sentenced to death by courts martial held at Hazebrouck. I was stupified as the adjutant droned out each man's name, rank, unit and offence, followed in each case by the words, 'and the sentence was duly carried out'. The hour and date of the execution were also read out.

6 Le Touquet trenches

Next day, Tuesday 21 June 1915, the battalion marched to Armentières and, after handing in our packs to the Quartermaster's stores, we entered the trenches for the first time. We took over from Princess Patricia's Canadian Light Infantry Regiment, who stayed with us for instruction purposes for a day. I was glad when they finally left us, for the front line was jammed with men, leaving no space to get out of the way for a rest. The Canadians were a tough crowd and I felt a mere slip of a lad beside some of them.

The line at this part took its name from the nearest village, le Touquet, which was close to the Franco–Belgian frontier. Like everything else in life, I soon found there was a routine or system to be followed in trench warfare. If the routine was upset by the outbreak of fighting, it was resumed when the fighting ceased. I learnt that the front-line soldier was only concerned with the matter of a hundred yards or so on either side of him. His prime interest was to know all about that piece of land stretching between his part of the trenches and the German trenches in front of him—No Man's Land. He should know the exact distance across No Man's Land, any weaknesses in the barbed-wire defences and the position of any ground features, such as ditches, buildings and shell craters. Careful scrutiny by day, usually with the aid of a periscope, should provide him with a complete mental picture for use in the night hours.

For convenience, it may be said that the day really began at stand-to. Past experience had shown that the danger period for attack was at dawn and dusk, when the attacker, having the initiative, could see sufficiently to move forward and cover a good distance before being spotted. About half an hour or so before dawn and dusk the order, 'Stand to', was given and silently passed through the length of the battalion front. In this way the whole Allied front line system became alerted. Sleepers were roused, and the front trenches were speedily manned ready for any move by the enemy. Sentries stood on raised fire-steps, peering over the parapet across No Man's Land, towards Jerry's lines. The rest of the lads quietly relaxed as they puffed at a pipe or fag, but no matches were used in darkness. A simple lighter which sparked off a thick corded wick into a smouldering glow was a popular substitute for matches. The origin of the unlucky third light from one match probably started in the South African War, but soldiers in all wars are superstitious and will not go out of their way to offend the gods.

An officer hurries along the trench to see that everyone is in a state of readiness and NCOs move about keeping a watchful eye on their particular section. Suddenly a German machine gun, pre-set before darkness to fire on our parapet, lets rip a devilish traverse, which skims the topmost sandbags. Dirt is flung into faces and foul language seethes through everyone's lips—'the bastard!' Not far off a Vickers gun returns the hate at an appreciably faster tempo as it shoots a hundred rounds or so across No Man's Land. Although there is no special cause for alarm, intermittent rifle fire develops, as if to let Jerry know we are wide awake and it's no bloody use his starting anything. Jerry responds likewise, for it is the morning hate. The whole process is rather like the early bird who starts his song in the dawn and is followed by rival songsters, the chorus gradually dying away when full daylight comes. There were not many birds near the trenches at le Touquet except an occasional owl. Just after dawn one day an owl came and perched on the wire in front of me, and I shot it, a stupid and senseless thing to do which I have always regretted. Before enlistment I had never noticed the splendour of dawn, but from the first moment of light in the east on those fine June days I watched every minute of change with wonderment as the sun crept up behind the German lines.

When daylight came the order, 'Stand down', passed along the line. Tension slackened, but sentries still kept watch by periscope or by a small mirror clipped to the top of a bayonet. After the dangerous hours of the night—or so they seemed to me in those early days—a cautious peer over the parapet revealed pleasant country with not a great deal of war damage except near the enemy trenches. Wisps of smoke at several points showed that Jerry was making his breakfast. Things were peaceful, although a sniper's shot broke the silence occasionally. Always there was the sniper, the loneliest and deadliest combatant in trench warfare, lurking like a jackal ready to strike.

It was time for our own breakfast and each section made its own little fire. Charcoal was the official fuel, but supplies were few and far between. Plundering for wood was a regular chore, but we never failed to produce a fire, slivering the wood with bayonets or jack-knives to reduce the smoke. Soon the pungent whiff of bacon wafted around and life seemed good when billycans were filled with a fresh brew of tea. Breakfast over, there was not long to wait before an officer appeared with details of the duties and fatigues to be performed. Weapon cleaning and inspection, always a prime task, would soon be followed by pick and shovel work. Trench maintenance was constant, a job without an end. Owing to the weather or enemy action, trenches required repairing, deepening, widening and strengthening, while new support trenches always seemed to be wanted. The carrying of rations and supplies from the rear went on interminably.

The trenches at le Touquet were in a very good condition, in parts almost like demonstration models. About six feet in depth from the top of the parapet, they were floored with duckboards, and were wide enough for two men to pass comfortably. A fire-step a foot or so high ran along each section of trench, enabling troops to adopt a good firing position in case of attack. The few dugouts that there were afforded very little more protection than a shell-hole. Most of them were just excavations at the bottom of a trench sufficient to crawl into and stretch out for sleep. The entrance was propped up with a bit of light timber, with sacking draped across to black out candle-light. In spite of the coffin-like dimensions, four men would squeeze in and be thankful for it. For the first few nights in one of these traps I was in a funk, fearing to doze off in case the sentry dozed off too, my arms curled through the sling of my rifle, just in case. I dreaded the thought that I might be caught unawares if a swarm of Jerries rushed our trenches in the darkness. There were latrines at intervals along the line, which generally took the form of small culs-de-sac cut in the back of the trench. The sites were shifted when necessary, as Jerry snipers watched them very closely for the careless. Many a poor Tommy met his end in a latrine sap.

One of the first casualties in 13 Platoon was a lad named Carroll. It was said that quite suddenly, and for no apparent reason, he stood exposed above the parapet in broad daylight, shouting and waving his arms about. What possessed him to do such a thing, against all the warnings and training that we had had drummed into us? I can only imagine that some kind of mental unbalance came over him. Jerry picked him off quickly through the head.

After a few days the battalion moved out of the le Touquet sector into trenches at Ploegsteert, commonly called 'Plug-street'. Here we had our first taste of German artillery fire. The first indication was the sound of four deep booms, which seemed to come from well behind the enemy lines. In a few moments I became aware of pulsating rushing sounds, increasing in power and intensity. The threatening noise struck equally between my ears, and I knew instinctively that the shells were heading in my general direction. The final vicious swipes of the projectiles as they rushed to earth turned my stomach over with fear, which quickly vanished when four hefty explosions occurred in some ruined houses a hundred yards to the rear.

This experience made me realise the value of a good pair of ears. Later on, keen eyesight and practice enabled most of us in clear weather to pick out howitzer shells in the air, thus giving us a split second's grace to decide which way to dart for cover. The

German 5.9 shells weighed about a hundred pounds, and were generally referred to as 'coal-boxes' or 'Johnsons' (after Jack Johnson) owing to the black smoke they gave off when bursting. Jerry artillery had an unpleasant habit of dispatching them in fours. 'Plugstreet' was about a mile inside the Belgian frontier and there had been severe fighting there shortly before our arrival, but on the whole things were quiet for us.

7 Armentières

On 6 July the battalion was relieved and marched to Armentières on the French side of the frontier, where we were billeted in the Blue Blind Factory. Conditions there seemed very much like Aldershot to me, for although we had tasted trench life and suffered some casualties, we were chased about drilling and training again. At the factory gates women sold delicious-looking pastries, and it was agony continually passing them without any money in my pocket. I never did have one of those pastries, which I've always felt sad about.

Armentières had a special appeal because of the legend of 'Mademoiselle from Armenteers', which was immortalised by the Old Contemptibles' song. Not long ago there was talk of erecting a statue of the famous lady to commemorate the fiftieth anniversary of her reincarnation. The tune of the song was believed to be popular in the French army of 150 years ago, and the original words told of the encounter of an inn-keeper's daughter, named Mademoiselle de Bar le Duc, with two German officers. During the Franco-Prussian war of 1870, the tune was resurrected, and again in 1914 when the Old Contemptibles got to know of it.

A bathing parade was organised before we returned to the trenches, and we marched to Pont de Nieppe and bathed in the river Lys. Major Watson, the battalion second-in-command, was in charge. In the warm summer evening we sported in the water like kids without a care. The war seemed far off, yet the line was but a mile away. The major blew his whistle for 'All out'. When we were dressing someone remarked, 'Where's the sergeant?' He was tangled in the reeds at the bottom of the river ten feet down. I believe his name was Williams. A number of us dived in and searched around but the thick weeds were too baffling. Two French watermen arrived with a punt and carefully dragged a grappling iron across the spot where the sergeant was last seen. At last the iron caught on the bulge of an ankle and up came the poor fellow, black with mud. His face and body were lacerated by the grappling iron. Artificial respiration was given but without success. I remember the major placing the inside of his gold cigarette case over the sergeant's mouth for traces of breath, but there were none.

After a rest of five days we returned to the le Touquet sector and stayed for ten days. Things were very quiet and at times life seemed almost pleasant, mainly because the weather was perfect. Early one morning I was startled to hear the sound of a trumpet, followed by the cry 'Dailee Mail! Dailee Mail!' and sure enough there was a French boy of about twelve selling papers a week old. How he got as far as the front line without being turned back nobody knew. The military situation at le Touquet was curious, for it seemed as if both sides, the Germans and ourselves, had tacitly agreed that this part of the line should be labelled 'Quiet', it being understood that if one side started up any bloody nonsense, then the other would follow suit. And that's how it was for days on end, except for snipers. Jerry was about a hundred and fifty yards away and behaving himself, but the usual machine-gun duels at stand-to went on.

8 The passing of Bill

Lulled by the quietness, someone is foolish and carelessly lingers with his head above the top of the parapet. Then, like a puppet whose strings have suddenly snapped, he crashes to the bottom of the trench. There is no gradual falling over, but instant collapse. A Jerry sniper with a telescopic sighted rifle, nicely positioned behind the aperture of an armoured plate, has lain patiently, for hours perhaps, watching our parapet for the slightest movement. His shot is successful and a Tommy is breathing his last, not quite lifeless, but dying. The back of the cranium is gone, and the grey brain flecked with red is splashed out.

A pal of mine named Bill Bailey (his real name) died in this way. There were four of us in a short section of trench, Bailey, Marshall, myself and another. It was early morning and stand-to was over. The fire was going nicely and the bacon was sizzling. I was sitting on the firestep. Just as I was about to tuck in Bill crashed to the ground. I'll never forget the sound of that shot as it found its billet. In trenches, sounds are trapped to a certain extent and take on a special quality. Several times I noted the similarity of sound when bullets found their mark in the head. An acoustic expert could no doubt give a reason for this. A moment before, Bill had been talking to us, and now, there he was, breathing slightly, but otherwise motionless. I rushed round the traverse and yelled, 'Pass the word along for stretcher-bearers!' We waited for them to come and for decency's sake put some bandages round Bill's head to hide the mess. Marshall and I volunteered to carry him to the first-aid post, and the bearers were glad enough to let us. Bill was a big chap and it was exhausting work carrying him down the narrow twisting communication trench. The battalion doctor was in attendance at the first-aid post. 'He can't last long,' he said, and so we left Bill, who died later that morning. When we got back to the front line we were both ravenous with hunger. My bacon and bread was on the fire-step, but covered with dirt and pieces of Bill's brain. I inspected the front of my tunic and trousers and there were more bits there; my boots were sticky with blood.

I felt the passing of Bill acutely, as it was the first time a pal had been struck down beside me. It was a shock to realise that death could come from nowhere without actual fighting. During the ten-day spell in that quiet sector, the battalion lost two or three men every day by Jerry sniping, none surviving. A very tall captain came from divisional HQ; he was sniped almost as soon as he arrived. Men approaching six feet or more in height began to realise they were in grave danger every minute, unless they took the utmost care and crouched low when moving about. Little chaps were at a distinct advantage so far as sniping was concerned. In fact, small men were the ideal size for trench warfare. Even when attacking, a little chap's frontage could be but two-thirds that of a big fellow, but as most Tommies agreed, 'If it's got your bloody number on it, there's nothing you can do about it.' The sniper war was not all one-sided, for our own snipers were achieving good results. One or two of them had been supplied with elephant guns powerful enough to pierce Jerry armoured plates.

The CO was worried about the sniping fatalities, and a general strengthening of parapets took place after dark. The protective strength of a parapet depended on what sort of earth it was made of. I see from an old notebook I have kept that the penetrative powers of a .303 bullet are as follows: clay 60 inches, earth 40 inches, loose sand 30 inches, sandbags 18 inches, oak 38 inches, dry turf 80 inches. This was just school stuff, and I don't remember my officer instructing that a parapet should be a certain thickness because of its nature. Experience was the best teacher, and our spell at le Touquet taught us the value of strong and well-maintained trenches, with special attention being paid to the parapets.

On 16 July 'D' Company went into reserve trenches at le Bizet, a smashed-up little village astride the frontier. The customs post was abandoned, but a few die-hard villagers remained in the ruined houses. Not having been abroad before, it intrigued me to be popping in and out of France and Belgium several times a day, for our section was within a few yards of the frontier. A salvo of coalboxes landed in the village with regular frequency, usually on the hour. An old man who lived in the cellar of his battered house earned a few francs cutting hair. Needing a crop, I went to his place one afternoon. When I called him he came up from the cellar with surprising speed and quickly ploughed a furrow up the back of my head with the clippers. At that moment we heard the approach of a salvo. The old chap vanished without a word, leaving me in the chair. The shells roared overhead and exploded nearly a quarter of a mile off. After the crumping detonations had died away, I yelled out, hoping to get the job completed, but the only reply was, 'Fini. Fini.' My pals heaped ridicule on me with my unfinished haircut, and it was some time before the crop was completed.

My platoon was later billeted in the barn of a fine old red-bricked farm on the outskirts of the village alongside a magnificent avenue of trees, a number of which had been struck down by enemy shells. The farm buildings were little damaged, but the owners had left. One night, when I was on sentry duty, I stood in the avenue of trees, which seemed to loom up in the darkness to the sky itself. Behind a brick wall at my back the platoon was sleeping. It was chilly, and the rattle of machine-gun fire from the trenches half a mile away sounded very close. Opposite me, across the avenue, I could just make out the outline of a crucifix and shrine.

Brilliant flashes suddenly lit the sky behind the German lines. Within a second or so came the sound of four consecutive booms from the howitzer battery which had fired. Quickly the approaching coal-boxes tuned in midway between my ears and I knew I was in for trouble. There was a shallow trench beside me. As I flung myself into it the shells rushed to the ground, one of them striking a tree fifty feet away. The violence of the explosion and the crashing down of the top half of the tree turned my insides over and deafened me. When I stood up it was difficult to control the trembling in my knees.

Brutally aroused from slumber, the platoon swarmed out of the barn to gaze at the stricken giant. Daylight came, revealing the top of the forty-foot stump spread out like a fan of huge splinters. The severed top drooped to the ground, linked to the stump by a single splinter. The crucifix opposite lay on the ground. One of its legs was smashed. Several more of those fine trees were bashed down before we left the area, for Jerry had a mania for knocking over anything that had the makings of an observation post overlooking his trench system.[1] Le Bizet church tower suffered in this way, and on one occasion a shell passed through a previous shell hole in the tower, exploding on the inside, a good example of German ballistic ability.

We went back to the trenches at le Touquet. The fine weather was still holding out, and Marshall and I soldiered along together. When the urge for arts and crafts made itself manifest we got boyish satisfaction out of making replicas of regimental cap badges. Melting the lead content of several bullets, we poured the boiling liquid into a mould made by pressing a badge on the clay bottom of the trench. The new brightness of the moulded badges was something created, however trifling. Often we did our sentry duty together, sharing a tin of bully or a tasty morsel, for we were always hungry. If either saw that the other was nodding off he would give him a good nudge to remove the

---

[1] In 1958 I passed through le Bizet on a tour from Ostende to Paris. I was surprised and delighted to find that the avenue of trees was almost restored to its former beauty. Forty-three years had passed.

THE PASSING OF BILL   29

constant fear of being caught.

Knocking out German observation mirrors was another exciting though dangerous pastime. We had discovered that Jerry was using big mirrors instead of periscopes. One bright evening with the sun behind our backs, we saw the movements of the Germans reflected in a mirror as they passed in front of it. The mirror was perched at an angle on top of their parados (the mound along the back of the trench) and directed towards our lines. A hit was recorded by a brilliant flash of reflected light as the mirror burst into fragments. We had several successes in this way, but our irritating tactics came to an abrupt end one evening when a sniper missed Marshall by just a few inches. Thoroughly scared by such a close shave, we packed up looking for Jerry mirrors.

Sometime in August the battalion had a disagreeable surprise sprung on it, for an order was given to resume full spit and polish of equipment. The luxury of not having to waste time and energy in senseless drudgery was to end. I don't know how high up the scale of rank the order came from. Whoever it was ignored the lessons of military history, which taught that troops should at all times be as inconspicuous as possible. Could it be that the top brass feared that they might lose proper control of the troops unless they reimposed the iron hand of 'Bull'? The polishing of brass gear in the trenches was the very negation of the superb camouflage of the khaki uniform. It was tantamount to deliberately discarding a natural protection. Looking at it today it seems crazy, but that's how it was and we had to grin and bear it.

Just before we left the le Touquet area, a German rifle-grenade killed RSM Annis while he was on a visit to the line. This was unfortunate indeed, for the RSM was not normally expected to leave battalion headquarters. His job was a disciplinary one when the battalion was not in the trenches, and then he came into his own. I found myself sad about his end, as I sometimes felt a certain warmth in his manner towards me. His place was taken by CSM Fulbrook of 'D' Company.

Our spells of twelve days in the front line, with breaks of four or five days' rest in Armentières, came to an end. It was the last week of September, and heavy artillery bombardments could be heard a few miles to the south. In a sense it was an advantage being a private for nobody told you anything. You just lived out a day-to-day kind of existence until things happened. It didn't do you any good to know that you were going to be in a great battle next Wednesday. I preferred not to have too much time to work myself into a state of wind-up.

9 The Battle of Loos

On 29 September we left the Blue Blind Factory at Armentières, marched to Steenwerck, and entrained for Fouquereuil. Next day we slogged it to Vermelles, a war-scarred little town in the coal-mining area close to the scene of the battle. The struggle which had begun five days before our arrival was working up to full cry. Salvoes of coal-boxes were crashing down nearby at the foot of the Vermelles-Hulluch road. Our artillery—the howitzers at our backs, and the field guns on both sides of us—was firing flat out. Its deafening thunder threatened the ear drums. It was inspiring, though uncomfortable, for soon eighteen-pounder shells were screaming just over our heads, an experience to which we were not yet accustomed.

Without much ado we were hustled into a communication trench and slowly moved towards the battle line. So this was real war. The other at le Touquet was just playing about by comparison. Yet our casualties there had been over seventy and nearly all fatal. What is seventy compared with what is going on here, I thought. The Loos attack was a combined Franco-British effort and was meant to push a salient in the German front line. There were over 60,000 British casualties and the battle lasted a month. At such high cost, with little or nothing to show for it, history has come to regard the attack as a failure. Neither General Joffre, the French GOC, nor Sir John French, the British GOC, added any lustre to his reputation from the Loos struggle. Not that it made any difference to us Tommies generally, but French was near the end of his command in France. He was replaced by Sir Douglas Haig in December 1915.

The battalion proceeded up the communication trench at a snail's pace, suffering casualties from shrapnel fire. As many troops were coming away from the front line as were going up.

Stretcher-bearers with the wounded, fatigue parties, telephone linesmen, runners and parties of relieved troops wended their way to the rear, jamming the narrow trench. The trench was parallel to the Vermelles-Hulluch road and was only a few yards from it. Bordered with tree stumps, it ran due east straight through to the village of Hulluch, which was just behind the German lines. A pall of black smoke hung over the village, which was being hammered by our guns. Wrecked war gear lay about on both sides as we edged forward, including field guns, limbers and dead horses by the score. Blown up by internal gases, their carcases were enormous, and when punctured by shrapnel or bullets the foulest stench poisoned the air.

At last we reached the top of a slope where the German front line had been before the attack. And there, stretching for several hundred yards on the right of the road, lay masses of British dead, struck down by machine-gun and rifle fire. Shells from enemy field batteries had been pitching into the bodies, flinging them into dreadful postures. As they mostly belonged to Highland regiments there was a fantastic display of colour from their kilts, glengarries and bonnets, and also from the bloody wounds on their bare limbs. The warm weather had darkened their faces and, shrouded as they were with the sickly odour of death, it was repulsive to be near them. Hundreds of rifles lay about, some stuck in the ground on the bayonet, as though impaled at the very moment of the soldier's death as he fell forward. In the distance, three kilometres south, and in the midst of concentrated shell bursts, I could discern the huge twin-tower steel structure known to the troops as 'Tower Bridge'. It stood at a pithead near the village of Loos and when captured by the British threatened the enemy as an observation post. It received a steady battering for a few days and its end was only a matter of time. One morning, when looking towards Loos, where a fierce rumpus was going on, I noticed that the tower had gone.

On the way up to the front line I carried two boxes of machine-gun ammunition, each containing 250 rounds, in addition to my rifle and equipment. It was a heavy load, but the fact that I had just been posted to the machine gun section kept me going, for I was anxious to show that I could cope.

10 The Hohenzollern Redoubt

When we reached the line, which was under considerable shell-fire, Lieutenant Clarke led 13 Platoon to the left along the front trench, passing dead and wounded Queen's men who had been knocked out within minutes of their arrival. Proceeding a short distance under heavy mortar fire, we gunners eventually took over a machine gun post in the Hohenzollern Redoubt. I can't remember the name of the regiment whose gun team we relieved, but they were off like a shot as soon as our Vickers gun was mounted in place of theirs. Who could blame them? By then, the Hohenzollern Redoubt had developed a reputation as one of the worst spots in the whole of the trench system. It was on the extreme left flank of the British offensive, though fierce fighting had been going on there a considerable time before the attack began. Our General Staff must have prayed that the redoubt would be captured in the early stages of the battle, and thus permit a further broadening of the salient which was to be driven through the enemy lines as far as Lens, the centre of the

mining area. But the British, with some assistance from the French, had failed to reach Lens. Moreover, the Germans were clinging tenaciously to the Hohenzollern Redoubt on their right flank, not yielding in spite of repeated assaults against them. The territory of the redoubt, a mass of pulverised dirt, covered no more than three or four acres, yet thousands fought and died there for months on end. I don't know who gave it the family name of the Prussian kings and emperors. Two of the trenches there, the scene of some of the bitterest fighting of the war, were called 'Big Willie' and 'Little Willie', in derisory reference to the Kaiser and his eldest son, the Crown Prince.

Le Touquet was generally considered to be a quiet front, and we soon found the Hohenzollern Redoubt to be the reverse. There was no let-up in the violence displayed by the enemy and

The attack on the Hohenzollern Redoubt, 13 September 1915. A cloud of smoke and gas can be seen in the centre and left of the picture, bursting shells in the centre and right. The British trenches and approaches are marked by the lines of excavated chalk. Units of the 46th (North Midland) Division managed to penetrate the redoubt but were driven back with heavy losses. *Imperial War Museum Q29001*

our troops, day or night. There were times later on in the winter when temporarily at least things were quiet on a good length of the front, but never in the redoubt. The place consisted of a number of huge mine craters, lying more or less between the German front line and our own. In some cases the edge of one crater overlapped that of another. The redoubt was scarcely a planned military work for it had been formed quite fortuitously. The craters almost fused both front lines together, so that there was a more or less constant dispute for the possession of No Man's Land. Companies of Royal Engineers, composed of specially selected British coal miners, worked in shifts around the clock digging tunnels towards the German line. When a tunnel was completed after several days of sweated labour, tons of explosive charges were stacked at the end and primed ready for firing. Careful calculations were made to ensure that the centre of the explosion would be bang under the target area. This was an underground battle against time, with both sides competing against each other to blast great holes through the earth above. With listening apparatus the rival gangs could judge each other's progress, and draw conclusions. A continual contest went on. As soon as a mine was blasted, preparations for a new tunnel were started. On at least one occasion British and German miners clashed and fought underground, when the final partition of earth between them suddenly collapsed.

The troops in the danger area withdrew when zero time for the detonation of one of our mines was imminent. If the resultant crater had to be captured, an infantry storming party would be ready to rush forward and beat Jerry to it. Some of the craters measured over a hundred feet across, descending funnel-wise to a depth of at least thirty feet. Several omnibuses could have been dropped into them with no trouble. At the moment of explosion the ground trembled violently in a miniature earthquake. Then, like an enormous pie crust rising up, slowly at first, the bulging mass of earth cracked in thousands of fissures. When the vast sticky mass could no longer contain the pressure beneath, the centre burst open, and the energy released carried all before it. Hundreds of tons of earth were hurled skywards to a height of three hundred feet or more, many of the lumps of great size. We held our breath as the deadly weight commenced to drop, scattered over a huge radial area from the centre of the blast. There was little to choose between a German mine and one of ours for death or injury from the falling mass was a risk to friend and foe alike. There was nowhere to run for shelter in the crater area. Troops just pinned themselves to the side of a trench, muttered a prayer of some sort, and cringed like animals about to be slaughtered.

Almost before the last lump dropped, the storming party rushed forward to capture the hot and smoking crater. The German flanks bristled with machine guns, and it was a safe bet that they would take a toll of some of our boys before they reached their objective. Those who made it literally dug in their toes to prevent themselves sliding backwards down the steep slope behind them. They lined the rim nearest the enemy, desperately prepared to die in defence of their meagre gain. It frequently happened that the capture of a crater brought the attackers less than a stone's throw from a crater strongly held by their opponents, twenty or thirty feet perhaps. A fierce bombing exchange would break out. Many of the bombs overshot the rim of the crater and, landing on the bottom, blasted fragments up the slope. Frantic efforts were made to stack a few sandbags at the back of our defenders to give them some protection. Both sides employed snipers at vantage points on the flanks and their deadly work added to the terror.

Because the front-line trenches and craters in the redoubt area were so close together neither side used artillery. The casualty rate rose rapidly for the first hour after the capture of a crater as alarm spread to neighbouring craters and trenches. Inspired by mutual hate and desperation, the volume of fire from short-range weapons increased, creating an almost impossible demand for stretcher-bearers. Crater fighters were considered to have a pretty mean chance of survival, twelve hours being reckoned as the limit a bloke could stand. Before starting a twelve-hour shift in a crater, each man had to complete a field postcard for his next of kin, leaving the terse message 'I am quite well' undeleted. What use this was I could never understand, for many a poor Tommy was dead within the hour.

According to my dictionary the definition of the word redoubt is, 'a detached outwork or fieldwork enclosed by a parapet without flanking defences'. If this is correct, then the Hohenzollern Redoubt wasn't a redoubt at all, for there was no enclosed

NOTHING is to be written on this side except the date and signature of the sender. Sentences not required may be erased.   If anything else is added the post card will be destroyed.

I am quite well.

I have been admitted into hospital
  { sick   } and am going on well.
  { wounded } and hope to be discharged soon.

I am being sent down to the base.

I have received your {
  letter dated_____
  telegram „ _____
  parcel   „ _____

Letter follows at first opportunity.

I have received no letter from you
  { lately.
  { for a long time.

Signature}
only.   }

Date_____

[Postage must be prepaid on any letter or post card addressed to the sender of this card.]

(25480) Wt.W3497-293 1,130m. 5/15 M.R.Co.,Ltd.

Field Postcard. Some men tried to send additional messages by deleting odd letters.   *Imperial War Museum Q71268* parapet. A better description of it would be, 'a bloody appendage to a trench sector'. Now that I have grown considerably older, with time to reflect, I still cannot understand what it was all for, but I have a strong suspicion that the Hohenzollern Redoubt was allowed to develop into a prestige cockpit which in fact had no military importance. Neither the Germans nor the British had the courage to say, 'Keep your blasted craters. You can have them. We will not waste any more lives uselessly in this way.' In spite of the bitterness of the long-drawn-out conflict, neither side secured any appreciable advantage over the other.

This, then, was the place where my fellow machine gunners and I had to spend the next eighteen days. Looking back, I realise how fortunate I was that the Number One in my gun team was Acting Lance-Corporal William Hankin, a brave cool customer from the forests of Hampshire. He was very fair, with hair almost white, and his cold grey eyes did more than anything else to help me control my fears. Nicknamed 'Snowy', he was a natural leader, and I treasure the memory of his friendship and courage. Our position on the fringe of the crater area was very exposed and in the daytime we concealed the gun under a bit of sacking. The field of fire was directed to cover any general attack on our front and, where conditions allowed, to subdue enemy attempts to capture craters. It took some time to get used to the possibility that the gun position was bang over the top of a German mine that might blast up at any moment. We feebly joked about flying high, but the prospect of making such a trip was far from amusing. Before darkness, a muzzle attachment was fitted to the end of the gun. This was a stovepipe extension to conceal sparks during night firing. Only enemy troops directly in front of the gun would see any sparks down the mouth of the pipe. In such circumstances, any dallying on their part in endeavouring to mark the position of the gun when firing could have fatal results.

Before continuing this narrative, I think a brief description of the Vickers gun is appropriate. This weapon proved to be most successful, being highly efficient, reliable, compact and reasonably light. The tripod was the heaviest component, weighing about 50 pounds; the gun itself weighed 28 pounds without water. In good tune the rate of fire was well over 600

Machine gunners filling the water jacket of their Vickers gun.
Imperial War Museum Q6317

rounds per minute, and when the gun was firmly fixed on the tripod there was little or no movement to upset its accuracy. Being water-cooled, it could fire continuously for long periods. Heat engendered by the rapid fire soon boiled the water and caused a powerful emission of steam, which was condensed by passing it through a pliable tube into a canvas bucket of water. By this means the gun could continue to fire without a cloud of steam giving its position away to the enemy

The Vickers gun is still used in many armed forces throughout the world, and there appears to be but little change in design from the model of fifty years ago. There were normally six men in a gun team. Number One was leader and fired the gun, while Number Two controlled the entry of ammo belts into the feed-block. Number Three maintained a supply of ammo to Number Two, and Numbers Four to Six were reserves and carriers, but all the members of a team were fully trained in handling the gun. In the trenches the Vickers was primarily used for defence, but it was also effectively used to assist an attack, by indirect or barrage fire, and to restrict and harass movement behind the enemy lines.

11 The 'Minnie' terror

Very soon came a new terror for us in the shape of huge mortar bombs. Following a dull thud from close behind the German trenches, we saw our first 'minnie', fired by a mortar gun that Jerry called a *Minnenwerfer* (mine-thrower). The missile was made from a steel drum, packed with high explosive and scrap iron. When fired, the thing sailed up in the air to a hundred feet or so with a lighted fuse trailing from it, describing a graceful curve as it travelled towards our lines. Which way will it go? This way or that way? There was a couple of seconds in which to decide. The Lord be with you if you misjudged and ran the wrong way. At last it descended, hitting the ground with a smack. Maybe there was a moment to draw breath and tense up. The explosion was devastating and the concussion threatened to tear one apart.

The devilish trail of a minnie curving towards him put fear in the heart of the bravest. Trenches were blasted into ruts. Incessant pick and shovel work was necessary to restore anything which resembled a parapet or parados. Men just disappeared and no one saw them go. A weary Tommy would scratch a hole in the side of the bottom of a trench to get out of the way of trampling feet. A minnie would explode, and the earth above him would quietly subside on him. Even if the exact spot was known, what was the good of digging him out? In one stroke he was dead and buried.

In those far-off days in the redoubt I knew that at any moment my life might be blotted out by a bullet crashing through my head, or by flying shell fragments rending me apart. In my fear,

I was permanently conscious that I was made with a brain box, heart, lungs and stomach, all available for the Almighty to decide what should be done with them.

The combined roar of minnies and of bombs exploding in the craters went on ceaselessly throughout our first night in the redoubt. We kept anxious watch, the Vickers loaded and ready to belt off 250 rounds. Once, a Jerry machine gun not more than eighty yards away opened fire, giving off a vivid spout of sparks. Snowy promptly silenced it, firing half a belt straight at it, and nothing more was seen or heard from it that night. Before dawn, stand-to was ordered, but we treated this as a poor sort of joke— night-time in the redoubt then was one long stand-to. Dawn came, and we looked a haggard lot as we munched bully and biscuits, washed down with tepid water. Tea-making was out, for the surest way to invite disaster was to start a fire. To the right of the Hulluch road a bombardment raged as the struggle round Loos continued. Nearby I could see a giant slag heap on the northern fringe of the redoubt, called Fosse 8, which was a few yards inside the German front line.

Marshall and I were sent to battalion HQ to collect rations; on our return we learned that the team was booked for a shift in one of the craters. And so we filled in the field postcards, declaring that we were all 'quite well', and with gun and gear crept into a flanking crater. There was barely enough room for the six of us on the lip, but we found some sandbags stacked behind us. At the bottom of the crater was a pile of corpses, some British, some German. I found it hard to keep my eyes away from them. I could not avoid them, no matter where I looked.

Around midnight a Very light distress signal shot up from one of our forward craters. This called for our gun to open fire and cover the ground between Jerry's front line and foremost crater. Snowy opened fire at once, sweeping the area with a full belt. Violent bombing had broken out. Although in the darkness we could see nothing, we had laid the Vickers on the enemy parapet at dusk, which ensured effective fire in the right quarter. For good measure Snowy ripped off a second belt, trimming the enemy parapet nearest the craters. Shortly after, we were relieved to see the all-clear signal go up.

We later heard that a Jerry attack had been beaten off after fierce hand-to-hand fighting. Moreover, through his prompt action, Snowy had knocked out a number of enemy reinforcements. Striking a blow at Jerry was a badly-needed tonic for our little unit. We had taken a lot of muck and had not been able to retaliate, owing to lack of a direct target. This enforced inactivity increased our fears, but when a call for aid came and the Vickers lashed out in answer our fears lessened and courage began to glow. Jerry was jumpy for the rest of that night, and kept bombing and firing rifle-grenades. The Queen's, who held four craters, replied with bomb for bomb. With occasional rips of machine-gun fire, accompanied by the roar of minnies dropping on our front line and support trenches, the dread sound of war was maintained. The Germans seldom used minnies against our craters, which were too close to their own.

It was an immense relief to get out of the crater at the end of our shift. We had been lucky. Because our position was on a flank, any rifle-grenades which had come our way had overshot to the back of the crater. In a sense, though, we were going from the frying pan into the fire, for we were back in the minnie area again. In twelve hours another spell of crater duty awaited us. In the meantime, the miners worked furiously digging their tunnels. Fatigue parties sweated as they dragged out masses of excavated earth and scattered it far and wide after dark.

Our mortar men did their best to counter the dreaded minnies, but their efforts were feeble by comparison, as the bombs used only weighed about 60 pounds. 'Toffee Apples' we called them. The stick part was a rod of metal an inch or more thick which was stuck in the barrel of the mortar gun, with the apple, which was as big as a football, protruding. When fired, the bombs would sail head over heels towards Jerry but, strangely, the stick very often came flying back, and caused quite a few casualties. It was not until a year later, with the appearance of the Stokes mortar gun, that our mortar gunners beat Jerry to the punch. A good crew on this revolutionary weapon could get nine bombs in the air before the first one struck the ground.

The days passed, and on 5 October we heard the depressing news that our divisional commander, Major-General Wing, had been killed at the foot of the Hulluch road near Vermelles. The general was on horseback with his escort of two lancers, when a coal-box struck in their midst. I knew little about generals then, but I was sorry that our leader should be killed in this way. To us in the Hohenzollern Redoubt the loss was a real and disturbing thing. Several years after the war a cigarette firm issued a series of cigarette cards, depicting the badges of army divisions in the Great War. The card for the 12th Division showed the ace of spades, and the short history stated that, 'The Division earned the unusual and melancholy distinction of losing its commander, Major-General F. D. V. Wing, CB, CMG, killed in action.' I presume that the quotation given was supplied by the War Office. Survivors of the 12th Division might be forgiven for hoping and trusting that there are other official distinctions included in the division's record of battle, less unusual and melancholy than that of losing its general. At least it indicated that few divisions lost their commanders, mainly I suppose because of the static kind of warfare. By comparison, during the Battle of Borodino in 1812, twenty-two Russian and eighteen French generals were killed. In the Second World War it was not uncommon for generals to be killed or captured. The command of the 12th Division was taken over by Major-General A B Scott, CB.

Prolonged exposure to siege warfare conditions of the type which prevailed in the Hohenzollern Redoubt seriously affected the morale and nervous systems of men not physically capable of endurance. If any poor devil's nerves got the better of him, and he was found wandering behind the lines, a not infrequent occurrence, it was *prima facie* a cowardice or desertion case. There was no psychiatric defence available to help save him from a firing squad. The RAMC knew little about mental distress brought on by the violence of war, or if they did, little was done about it. They recognised a shell-shock case, when a man loses control of his limbs, but what of the man who, although not a raving lunatic, loses control of his will? Psychiatry as a profession was unknown or else not officially recognised then. It is my considered opinion that some men who met their end before a firing squad would willingly have fought the enemy in hand-to-hand combat, but they simply could not endure prolonged shell and mortar fire.

There was a scarcity of water in the redoubt and shaving was not permitted for a period. Those with vigorous hirsute growth looked like cavemen. An intriguing rumour was afoot that the RSM was in trouble for shaving, but I never heard that he was put on a charge for disobeying an order. A shave lasted me ten days then, but Lamport of 13 Platoon, a big ginger chap, had a beard an army razor wouldn't touch. He led a hell of a life because of it.

Sharing out the rations for a small unit was a bit of a lottery, especially where tins of jam, bully beef, pork and beans, butter and so on were concerned. The share-out was seldom favourable to a six-man team. So far as I know there were no hard and fast rules regarding the quantity of each type of ration a man was entitled to. The Army Service Corps were the main distributors, but how much food actually arrived in the trenches depended on such things as transport, the weather and enemy action. Irregular appropriations were likely to be made *en route*. When casualties occurred the share-out was bigger, but only for a day or two. A bread ration was seldom seen in the redoubt. The hard biscuits which were issued must have been torture for men with false teeth, who had to soak them in water. Wrapping loose rations such as tea, cheese and meat was not considered necessary, all being tipped into a sandbag, a ghastly mix-up resulting. In wet weather their condition was unbelieveable, and you could bet that the rats would get at them first. Maconochie, a 'dinner in a tin', was my favourite, and I could polish one off with gusto, but the usual share-out was one tin for four men. Tinned jam was an important part of our diet, and in the early days always seemed to be plum and apple, made by a firm named Tickler. It was not popular, and a derisory ditty went like this:

> Tickler's jam, Tickler's jam,
> How I love old Tickler's jam,
> Plum and apple in a one pound pot,
> Sent from Blighty in a ten ton lot.
> Every night when I'm asleep,
> I'm dreaming that I am,
> Forcing my way through the Dardanelles,
> With a ton of Tickler's jam.

Soldiers' jam took on a new look when Australia supplied such varieties as Quince Conserve, Melon and Honey, and Pineapple. I do not recollect ever receiving an apple or an orange as part of my rations in France.

12 'Chatting'

On 18 October the battalion was relieved and trudged back to Verquin, a village near Béthune. We were done up and severely shocked by our experiences. That they were just the beginning of a long unknown period full of such happenings was a certainty. A full day's rest allowed us to clean up a bit, and to launch a full-scale attack on lice. I sat in a quiet corner of a barn for two hours delousing myself as best I could. We were all at it, for none of us escaped their vile attentions. The blighters lay in the seams of trousers, in the furrows of long woolly pants, and seemed impregnable in their deep entrenchments. A lighted candle applied where they were thickest made them pop like Chinese crackers. After a session of this, my face would be covered with small blood spots from extra big fellows which had popped too vigorously. My pals would look the same, as if some dreadful contagion had suddenly assailed them. In parcels from home it was usual to receive a tin of supposedly death-dealing powder or pomade, but the lice thrived on the stuff. Lice hunting was called 'chatting'. If a chap said he was going for a 'chat' we knew what he meant. The word sounds as if it originated in the Indian Army.

The battalion cooks got busy with the field-kitchens, and life began to glow in us with the sweet smell of bacon frying. A familiar cry I loved to hear was, 'Roll up for your dip!' This was the hot swimming bacon fat in which one could dip a slice of bread. Experience told me to drop everything and run like hell to get in quick. Sometimes the cooks poured an extra tin of condensed milk into the big dixies of tea. The toffee-like brew seemed delicious to my young palate. Bully beef stew, too, tasted jolly good when one hadn't had a hot meal for three weeks.

Three or four of us went to Béthune one evening. The estaminets were full of soldiery and were doing a roaring trade. Snowy and I got primed on *vin blanc*, and started to look for a house where rumour had it that certain ladies were available for two francs. The rumour was either false, or we were too stupid to find the place.

At a post parade I was delighted to receive a wrist watch from a dear aunt and uncle of mine. It was the first watch I had ever owned. My uncle Alfred, who knew that I had become a confirmed smoker, regularly sent me a hundred cigarettes a month. Cigarettes were as important as ammunition. A Tommy would ask for a fag when near death, as if it was some kind of opiate that relieved pain and smoothed the path to oblivion. I've no doubt at all that it did. A shortage of cigarettes was sheer agony, and I once tried smoking dried tea leaves rolled in brown paper. It was pretty horrible. Weekly rations usually included twenty, perhaps thirty, cigarettes per man but most Tommies relied on parcels from home for their main supplies. Relatives and friends must have made considerable sacrifices to do this for their loved ones. A funny character in 13 Platoon, Bill Collins, always rolled his own with a pungent dark shag, and used his cap as a cigarette case. His first fag-end after stand-down in the early morning had a rich aroma like a cigar. It was a treat to see the satisfaction he got from it. Once he gave me a couple of puffs and my head reeled.

It was about this time that a parcel arrived for a comrade in our gun team who had been wounded and who was then on his way to Blighty. So the parcel was opened and the contents shared amongst the rest of the team. They consisted of cigarettes, a big cake and some chocolate. There was a letter inside the parcel from the sister of the wounded man. Her name was Mary, and I wrote and gave her the news about her brother. I also told her that we had shared the contents of the parcel and that we hoped she wouldn't mind. Two or three weeks later a parcel arrived for me; it was from Mary. There was a letter, too, expressing the hope that the team would enjoy the parcel. That dear girl, who lived at Maryport, Cumberland, kept up her generosity for quite a while, until it became a pleasing subject of conversation. From time to time someone would remark, 'I wonder when we'll get the next parcel from Mary?'

On 26 October we returned to Vermelles. The Battle of Loos had petered out, but the noise of bombing in the redoubt area renewed the sensation of fear in the pit of my stomach. The Guards Division was in the neighbourhood, and the Prince of Wales was seen by some of the lads. For the first time I noticed members of the newly-formed Welsh Guards Regiment.

13 Fosse 8

We went up to the front line again, a little to the left of the redoubt. The dominating feature here was Fosse 8, a vast heap of coal waste about eighty to a hundred feet high, and, if my memory serves me, well over a hundred yards long. The two front lines were very close, less than a hundred yards apart; with the Fosse looming directly in front of us we felt naked and wide open to enemy observation. The black monster was a puzzle, yet only once did we catch a Jerry on it. Leaving it too late after first light, his silhouette was sharp and clear on the skyline, and that was the end of him. By the accuracy of his mortars and rifle-grenades, which were fired from the back of the Fosse, it was certain that the enemy kept observation on us from this huge mass, which seemed to tower over us.

The sniping too was deadly. Sometimes our artillery pounded the great lump, churning up huge clouds of black dust, and Jerry would lie doggo for a while. On humid days we could discern faint eddies of smoke puffing forward from machine guns firing from the bowels of the Fosse, no doubt dug in and camouflaged in some way. Screened behind a bit of sacking, Snowy would pump a long burst at the spot, the bullets tearing into the slag, ricocheting violently. Snowy's riposte was usually followed by Jerry rifle-grenades dropping dangerously close to our position. One nearly put paid to Snowy and me. We saw it a moment before it landed in front of the Vickers, and ducked. The gun was knocked over and two holes were pierced in the water jacket. Temporary repairs were made with moulding clay from the gun's first-aid kit, and a neat patch was put over the holes by the battalion armourer later on.

As we were on the fringe of the redoubt, the minnie threat extended to our area and many dead were churned up in bits and pieces. Every square yard of ground seemed to be layered with corpses at varying depths, producing a sickening stench. We would curtain off protruding parts with a sandbag, pinned to the side of the trench with cartridges. A swollen right arm with a German eagle tattooed on it used to stick out and brush us as we squeezed by, and once a head appeared which hadn't been there an hour before. When it was impossible to conceal them we'd chop off the putrid appendages and bury them. So long as we were alive we had to go on living, but it wasn't easy with the dead sandwiched so close to us. We took our meals and tried to sleep with them as our neighbours. Amid laughter and bawdy stories they were there.

In keeping with this almost sub-human way of life went the foul language which we used in nearly every sentence. I'm sure that half the time we didn't know we were swearing. It just came naturally, as if it was the proper way to talk. I often think that this bad habit was an unconscious protective shield to keep us from becoming crazy. To us, everybody in authority was a bastard of some kind, and the RSM, a decent bloke really, was the subject of many vain boasts to do him in at the first horrible opportunity. The enemy were always 'bloody bastards'. The supreme odium was to refer to someone as a windy bastard, which was, of course, just being bloody nasty, for without doubt we were all windy at some time or other, a few no doubt more windy than others. It must be acknowledged that in most of the situations that Tommies had to contend with, bad language was the only kind that made sense. The adjective derived from the four-letter word held pride of place in our limited vocabulary. 'Pass me that ——— pozzy', (jam) was considered proper English. A pent-up bloke felt good after delivering a particularly foul and original sentence, and his face would beam at the cheers which acclaimed his efforts.

Rats, too, were a powerful contributory cause of some of the language used. They bred by the tens of thousands and lived on the fat of the land. When we were sleeping in funk holes the things ran over us, played about, copulated and fouled our scraps of food, their young squeaking incessantly. There was no proper system of waste disposal in trench life. Empty tins of all kinds were flung away over the top on both sides of the trench. Teeming millions of tins were thus available for all the rats in France and Belgium in hundreds of miles of trenches. During brief moments of quiet at night, one could hear a continuous rattle of tins moving against each other—the rats were turning them over. What happened to the rats under heavy shell-fire was a mystery, but their powers of survival kept pace with each new weapon, including poison gas.

One night, with a big moon rising behind Jerry's line, I put a piece of cheese on the parapet, a black mountain against the moon's face. I cocked a revolver close to the bait and stood motionless. Rat after rat came in quick succession, took one sniff and died. At one time a sandbag full of peas hung from the vaulted roof in Vermelles brewery, a safe enough place we thought. When all were asleep, a rat stood on a man's head and tore at the bag. Suddenly a cascade of peas showered on the sleeper's face, and he woke up shouting and striking out in his alarm. Pandemonium and foul language spread through the vaults.

During the Loos battle there were always officers and men on duty of one sort or other a short distance behind the front line and when rats were spotted the news spread fast. Officers with revolvers and troops with rifles appeared on the scene eager to join in rat extermination. All except two of the rat holes were bunged up; a smoke bomb was poked into one and the other was left as an exit. When the rats began to pour out the hunt was on. Quite a few senior officers joined in the free-for-all, which at times was positively dangerous, but it was great fun.

After twelve days in the Fosse 8 area, the battalion was relieved and marched to the village of Sailly-Labourse. The usual cleaning up and 'chatting' preceded a bath, surely the funniest of a lifetime. Steam had been raised at the pit head of a coal mine. In a shed stood a number of huge vats about six feet high and eight across, each holding several hundred gallons of hot water of a murky hue. A short ladder leaned against each vat. The entire place was covered in coal dust and grime, and there was little room in which to move. We cared not a bit, and in we plunged. It was a riot. The noise rivalled a madhouse. An old French boiler-man who was in attendance never even smiled, probably thinking of the mess he would have to clear up later. The big laugh came when we were drying ourselves. Everybody had a black behind. At the finish we were as black as our divisional badge.

When in reserve, it was normal routine in the machine gun section to give guns, accessories and equipment a complete overhaul. Most of us were dedicated enthusiasts and strove to maintain the weapons at peak efficiency. Gun barrels had an average life of 18,000 rounds of firing, after which accuracy fell off. A spare barrel was carried for replacement when necessary.

At Sailly I was put on guard duty. It was early November and the nights were dark and cold. Flashes of light from the Hohenzollern Redoubt five kilometres east lit the sky. I could hear the deep roar of minnie bursts as I paced up and down outside a row of miners' cottages in which my companions were sleeping. At first light in the morning a party of a dozen men approached my post and turned off into the Annequin road, where there was a disused coal mine. Later on I heard a volley of shots. A rumour went round that two Tommies had been executed that morning. Rumours of that kind were generally based on fact. Somebody always got to know. Executions became the subject of much earnest conversation, especially when a list of names was published. Personally, I was horrified at this terrible military law, and I was scared stiff that one day I would be picked for a firing squad. Would I be able to shoot straight at another Tommy? To be honest, I don't think I would have refused. The code of slavish obedience to orders given, no matter what, was as strong in me as in all volunteers then. That was the important thing about the volunteer system fifty years ago. A man was challenged, not compelled, to fight for his country and all that entailed. A volunteer seldom failed to meet the challenge, because of an inborn pride at being a volunteer. It worked that way.

Our six days' rest passed in a flash and in no time we were back in front of Fosse 8. From the comparative seclusion of Sailly, we were pitched within a couple of hours into some kind of Dante's inferno again. A quick dispatch to kingdom-come hovered in the air for those with ill-fated regimental numbers. My diary says, 'Heavy shelling and mortars here. Very cold.' Winter clothing had not been issued and the nights were bitter. I was now Number Two in the gun team, Snowy being Number One. He kept the spare lock—a vital reciprocating part of the mechanism—in his trouser pockets to keep it warm, as the cold stiffened the oil on the moving parts. Every half-hour he whipped the lock out of the gun and substituted the warm one from his pocket.

When I was with Snowy I always felt confident. He set for me a standard of cool behaviour that I tried to imitate and profit by. He was an expert in his understanding of the idiosyncracies of the Vickers and in his marksmanship. Wielding an axe in his forester's job had developed a powerful pair of hands and forearms. He loved to exert his strength, especially on me. Without warning he'd grip my hand and squeeze. 'Handgrips with the Brandenburger' he called this manoeuvre, forcing me to yelp. He knew his Conan Doyle and H G Wells, and that made him a well-read man so far as I was concerned. Reciting heroic poetry was another of his likeable habits; to this day I can remember a good deal of 'King Robert of Sicily', which he declaimed in grand theatrical style, gestures and all. Many a time on watch together, and Jerry barely a hundred yards off, I'd say, 'What about a bit of King Robert, Snowy?' And he would oblige.

Only a strong man could be Number One. He carried the tripod, the heaviest item of equipment. At that time, each of us carried a rifle and 120 rounds of personal ammunition as well, and when we were moving under our loads the rifles seriously hampered our passage in the narrow trenches. This was put right later when the Machine Gun Corps was formed and revolvers were issued.

Our relief came at the end of a ten-day spell in front of Fosse 8, but we left one of the team behind. A minnie blast buried him and although we dug him out quickly his neck was broken. As we tramped back to Vermelles down a communication trench called 'Wing's Way', after our late commander, we were a quiet lot. We slept in the brewery vaults, and felt safe enough to enjoy a good night's rest. The next morning, as we stood ready to march off to Sailly, a coal-box plunged into the brewery ruins and killed a sergeant as he emerged from the vaults. There was not a scratch on him—concussion had done it.

We spent a few days at Sailly, and on 22 November the battalion marched via Béthune to a hamlet near Lillers called Ecquedecque, a total of 20 kilometres. Each step we took was in the right direction, away from the war area. And as we marched our spirits soared, in spite of our 80-pound load. The senior officers, as befitted their station, sat astride well-groomed horses. The troops marching immediately behind the horses kept a wary eye on their hindquarters. Any sign of a tail elevation was quickly noted and evasive action was taken when necessary, accompanied by mock cries of alarm. Occasionally the riders would dismount to stretch their legs. Immaculate as always, with spurs a-jingling, 'D' Company CO, Captain Hull, would scrutinise the ranks and pick up somebody with a button unfastened on his tunic, or similar trifle. This would be the signal for the CSM and sergeants to get all pepped up and start yelling commands. 'That man there!' 'Put yer hat straight!' 'Pick 'em up, left right, left right!' There was no visible reaction against all this, but every Tommy muttered 'Bastards!' under his breath, I'll wager.

Along the straight cobbled roads we marched. The tree-lined sides stretched ahead, the perspective drawing them together in a never-changing V for a couple of kilometres or so. There would be a slight change of direction and straight ahead another taunting V. As the distance increased, so likewise did the weight of our packs, and the more cruel the cobble-stones became to our feet. Although it was late in the year, it was good to see the clean hedgeless countryside, now clear of the harvest. We passed many farms where threshing was in progress. I remember seeing a handsome Percheron horse penned in a sloping escalator affair, using his great strength and weight to turn the wheels of the threshing machine. It was a strange and fascinating sight as we slogged along. In the villages big dogs were pulling small carts; there was one in a treadwheel, walking fast but getting nowhere. Everything was peaceful, as the peasants went about their work in the age-old way.

To the sound of mouth-organs playing, the marching column would break into song, each platoon or company singing a different tune perhaps. Colonel Bogey was second only to lowbrow rhymes about the war, sung to well-known hymn tunes with words varied to taste. One rhyme about the Army Service Corps (sometimes referred to as 'Alley Sloper's Cavalry') was sung to the hymn tune 'The Church's One Foundation', and went as follows:

> We are King George's army,
> We are the ASC.
> We cannot fight, we cannot march,
> What —— good are we?
> But when we get to Berlin,
> The Kaiser, he will say,
> 'Hoch, Hoch, Mein Gott,
> What a bloody fine lot
> Are the boys of the ASC!

A special favourite of mine when marching was a kind of recitative. Suddenly, during a lull in the singing, a voice from somewhere in the ranks would begin a solitary declamation in mock dramatic style:

Recitative:	Today's my daughter's wedding day, Ten thousand pounds I'll give away.
Chorus (with gusto):	Hooray! Hooray!
Recitative:	On second thoughts, I think it best I'll store it in the old oak chest.
Chorus (with jeers):	You stingy old bastard! You dirty old bleeder!

All within earshot joined in the chorus, the last line being delivered with professional clarity and venom. I had a warm regard, too, for the humour of the following:

> Far, far from Ypres I long to be,
> Where German snipers can't pot at me.
> Deep in my dugout, where the worms creep,
> Waiting for sergeant to sing me to sleep.

The battalion stayed in Ecquedecque for fourteen days, during which time the machine gun sections had special intensified training. There were now four Vickers guns to be manned, and plans were afoot to amalgamate with the other three machine gun sections in the 37th Brigade. When joined together, the sixteen guns would form the armament of the 37th Machine Gun Company of the Machine Gun Corps. Similar amalgamations were taking place throughout the overseas army forces, while in England new machine gun companies were being formed and attached ready-made to new divisions.

14 Givenchy

On 6 December we marched back to Béthune, stopping the night in an empty tobacco factory. Next day we took over a trench sector in the Givenchy area, five kilometres north-west of the Hohenzollern Redoubt. The trenches were full of liquid mud, which reached up to our knees. With no proper dugouts and no dry place to sleep, we were soon in a wretched state. It rained cats and dogs, and the nights were pitch dark and bitterly cold. On gun duty the hours dragged by with excruciating tedium and hunger. My thoughts would drift to a spot where a punctured tin of condensed milk was concealed in a cavity, and I would speculate on the risk involved in filching a swig without my companions knowing. Being young I was ravenous for sweetness.

The Givenchy sector had all the elements of a most unpleasant spell: Prussian troops facing us across No Man's Land, minnies and water-logged trenches. The Prussians—I find it strange to think of them as East Germans today—no doubt regarded themselves as the crack German infantry, with some justification perhaps, for they were the most belligerent of all the Jerry troops. Saxons, by contrast, were the quietest, and wouldn't go out of their way to foment any strafing. Did the Prussians know that we were new arrivals, and decide to give us a bit of a reception? For two days they kept up a torment of minnies and rifle-grenades. At first light on the third day, Snowy and I saw a sheet of white material stretched taut, and well in front of the enemy wire, on which was painted, 'Onward to Paris'. To register suitable defiance and disdain of the Prussian boast, Snowy raked the sheet with a full belt, blasting the message and carving the material to ribbons. This affront aroused the ire of the Prussians, and over came the minnies with a vengeance. Stand-to was on, and sporadic rifle-fire by both sides soon reached fusillade proportions. But it was nothing more than a fierce morning hate and after ten minutes it died down.

Bust-ups with the Prussians would start on the slightest pretext. Although a lot of ammunition may have been wasted, it was good for morale to have a bang in Jerry's direction, if only with a rifle, and it made the noise of war. We knew he was just across No Man's Land in large numbers—his volume of rifle-fire told us that—and he had to be kept there. Except when in the craters, one might not see a single Jerry for days on end. Fierce exchanges of fire caused casualties, chiefly by minnies. A direct hit on a short section of trench would wipe out everybody in it. Bullets skimming the top of the parapet took on lightning changes of direction after they had richocheted. In a crowded trench it was not uncommon for two or even three men to be hit by a ricochet. Jarvis was shot clean through the neck by one when standing close beside me. He bled severely, and when he was carted off we felt sure he was a goner. But, far from pegging out, he was sent no further than the base hospital. The bullet had passed through his neck without rending a vital part and, the wound quickly healing, he was back in the front line in a few weeks. This was tough luck really, as he deserved a spell in Blighty.

Some men seemed to get wounded as soon as they arrived in the trenches. One Tommy I knew had three separate wounds all received in the front line, and his total service in the trenches was but ten days in all. He got his third wound when mounting a ladder to go over the top in an attack. He slipped backwards and was impaled on the bayonet of the Tommy behind him, causing a deep and ugly gash, which sent him to Blighty. The prospect of collecting a 'Blighty one' was the fond hope of most men, but wishful thinking in this connexion usually excluded maiming by lumps of shrapnel. Only bullet wounds were acceptable.

Our gun team moved a short distance away to Marie Redoubt, a non-crater affair attached to the front trench. An artillery observation officer approached our gun position and proceeded to give fire directions by telephone to his eighteen-pounder battery in the rear. The battery opened fire and shells screamed just over the top of us, crashing into some brickwork inside Jerry's front line. Sixty or seventy shells were fired, after which the officer packed up and cleared off to the rear. As expected, we hadn't long to wait for enemy retaliation by whizz-bangs, and several of the Queen's were killed and wounded by direct hits on our trench. This kind of thing happened frequently. At a Tommy's level some of our artillery shooting seemed crazy, maybe because we didn't appreciate the significance of the target, but more probably because we feared we would get the dirty end of the stick, as we invariably did.

One rainy night it fell to me to draw the team's rations from battalion HQ at Cuinchy. We cut cards for the job and I drew the ace, which was low. I wandered about in the darkness without a clue as to my whereabouts. Suddenly I saw a faint light in a ruined building, and a savoury odour wafted towards me. Investigating further, I found to my delight that I had stumbled across a kind of soup kitchen. The Tommy in charge was stirring a copperful of 'Shackles' (soup made from the very dregs of army cooking) with a big stick. I must have looked in need of extra nourishment for he said, 'D'yer want a drop, son?' 'Yes, please,' I replied, 'if you can spare it.' The warmth and zest from that beefy liquid, unexpected as it was, compelled me to accept a second bowlful, which I drank with the same enthusiasm as the first. When I returned with the rations I upset my pals a little by bragging about the soup. The next time rations had to be fetched everybody volunteered to go. The name Cuinchy reminds me that Captain Robert Graves in his book *Goodbye to All That* mentions that on his return from Cuinchy he partook of a special dinner. It consisted of fish, new potatoes, green peas, asparagus, mutton chops, and strawberries and cream, washed down with three bottles of Pommard. Still, I doubt whether he enjoyed that meal more than I did the soup on that cold wet night.

At Givenchy I had my first issue of rum. It was not enough to get me mad and make me want to take on the whole German army, but it was jolly welcome for all that. It must have been proof spirit for its fire nearly choked me. It was generally thought that the Jocks were more favourably treated in rum issues than the English. I'm sure there was something in this, especially when the Jocks were going to attack. Rum issues to our gun team were a hit or miss affair. Being a small unit, more often than not we were overlooked. Senior NCOs knocked the stuff back all right, drinking far more than their ration. The song about rum wasn't cooked up for nothing. To the tune of 'Though your Heart may Ache Awhile, Never Mind' one verse ran:

> If the sergeant drinks your rum,
> Never mind!
> And your face has lost its smile,
> Never mind!
> He's entitled to a tot,
> But not the bleedin' lot,
> If the sergeant drinks your rum,
> Never mind!

Close to our gun position on the right was the La Bassée canal, which ran due east through the German lines. The two paths were used as thoroughfares for troops and transport. Jerry knew this and at times played havoc with coal-boxes. One day a horse took fright, ran off and fell down the mouth of a well. He was stuck half way down with his nose at ground level. How do you get a horse out of a well without tractors or mechanical lifts? A crowd of Tommies who had gathered (I was one of them) solved the problem by starting to dig about twelve feet from the well, gradually working down towards it. We dug furiously, but we had ample reliefs to lessen the task. Very soon the side of the well was breached to a depth of six feet, and the animal was hauled out. Just before we left Givenchy the Royal Engineers blew up a huge mine under the German line, but no attempt was made to occupy it.

The battalion returned to Béthune and rested in the tobacco factory. It was sheer luxury to have a dry clean floor to sleep on. The cooking arrangements were good too. 'Burgoo' (porridge) before the breakfast fry-up, and 'spotted dog' (currant pudding) with dinner, were welcome fillers. The factory was near the centre of the town and a major attraction was the Red Lamp establishment, authorised with Anglo-French consent. Captain Graves has mentioned a Blue Lamp establishment for officers, but I never thought of officers in that connexion, and I don't remember seeing a Blue Lamp.

The Red Lamp was situated at the end of a cul-de-sac which led off the town's main square. The night I took a look was quite a shock to me. The place was jammed by a mass of khaki soldiery, spilling out into the square. There were well over a hundred and fifty men waiting for opening time, singing 'Mademoiselle from Armenteers' and other lusty songs. Right on the dot of 6 pm a red lamp over the doorway of the brothel was switched on. A roar went up from the troops as they lunged forward towards the entrance. At that period in my youth I certainly had no idea that the carnal desires of men went to such lengths. A bloke told me that one chap had his leg broken in the rush a week before, and I could well believe it. Madame Tellier, de Maupassant's famous character in his story *Madame Tellier's Establishment*, would have been horrified to witness such behaviour outside her place; or would she? I tagged on behind the crowd, irresistibly drawn.

Eventually I found a seat in the bar and looked about me. There were several heavyweight chuckers-out, all wearing PT instructor's jerseys, which I swear had at one time been in some British quartermaster's store. They looked formidable with their big black moustaches and their hair plastered over their foreheads with a quiff. They laid their hands on the boys, sorting them out for the dames, who stood on the steps of a spiral stairway that led to the boudoirs above. As for the dames, poor dears, they seemed a jaded and worn-out lot. A couple of them were old enough to be grandmothers. Madame-in-charge, a big black-haired woman with a massive bosom, stood at the foot of the stairway, palm outstretched, demanding tribute of two francs from each candidate: one franc for madame, one franc for the dame.

It was said that Red Lamps were frequently inspected by RAMC doctors and the women medically examined. But many Tommies made random contacts with women in the back streets and picked up VD for their pains. These were the most unfortunate of men. Fifty years ago the disease was regarded as a dreadful and shameful contagion. Military authority subscribed to this view and dealt harshly with a Tommy VD case. He was clapped in a kind of prison hospital down at the base and treated as an outcast. Hard labour was his portion, with a court-martial hanging over his head. The substance of the charge against him was that by his action he had so disabled himself as to become a casualty. That was the predicament he was in, as we in the trenches understood it. The stigma was such that very few front-line Tommies, in spite of the misery and danger they had to endure, would have swapped places with a VD man at a base hospital.

15 Awash at Festubert

After four days' rest the battalion moved towards the trenches at Festubert. I always think of my time there as one of the worst of my experiences, not so much because of enemy action but because of the miserable conditions. To start with, the front-line area was flooded and the communication trenches had vanished under water. There was no front-line trench. Instead, earthworks, constructed of sandbags piled up on top of the original parapet, had been made. These earthworks or breastworks were like islands jutting out of the water, about twenty yards long, and spaced out every three or four hundred yards. A Vickers gun team was posted on each island to defend the line, while the rest of the battalion remained in the rear, clear of the swamp. Before we took over one of the islands, our gun team was issued with thigh-length rubber boots, which were excellent provided the water did not reach over the tops. In intense darkness, a guide led us towards the line. We left the firmness of the road and struck across country, encountering the first of a chain of duckboards strung out on supports above the water.

Lance-Corporal Snowy Hankin was Number One and carried the tripod; myself as Number Two carried the gun; and the rest of the team humped the remaining gear. Each man had his rifle and ammo, which further hampered his movements when balancing on the duckboards. It was stilly quiet, and the clatter we made must have been heard by Jerry. Suddenly a machine gun opened fire, the bullets passing about twenty yards to the right. The enemy gunner started a spraying action and bullets lashed all over the place. It was too much for us to stand up to, and to a man we leapt off our precarious perch into the drink and crouched as low as possible. It was a hellish few moments, but we all survived. The water poured into our boots and two poor devils fell over, completely immersed. In a flash we were reduced to a state of exasperating misery and discomfort. The gun team we relieved spoke in whispers, and told us they could hear the Germans talking. Wishing us a happy Christmas, they crept away like ghosts and we were left in the inky blackness. It was in fact 23 December 1915, and we were to be stuck on the island for four days.

We perched on a small strip of earth to avoid slipping into the water. The night was quiet, and when daylight came we realised there was barely four feet of cover. Bent nearly double, unable to stand, we waited as the hours dragged on, longing for darkness so that we could stretch our limbs a little. Watch was kept by periscope. Several times a sniper trimmed the top of the breastwork, making us sweat blood. The barbed wire in front was nearly submerged, but Jerry's wire was clear, as the ground was a few feet higher there.

It was Christmas Eve, and just after dark a second lieutenant came to visit us. I think his name was Clark. Among other

Machine gun post of the 62nd Battalion, Machine Gun Corps.
Imperial War Museum Q11088

things, he came to remind us that by order of the Commander-in-Chief there was not to be any fraternising with the enemy on Christmas Day. The whole world knew that on Christmas Day, 1914, there was some fraternising at one part of the line, and even an attempt at a game of football. Troops in the front line a year later were naturally speculating on whether a repeat performance would develop and, if so, where. Speaking for my companions and myself, I can categorically state that we were in no mood for any joviality with Jerry. In fact, after what we had been through since Loos, we hated his bloody guts. We were bent on his destruction at each and every opportunity for all the miseries and privations which were our lot. Our greatest wish was to be granted an enemy target worthy of our Vickers gun.

Sad it is for me to tell that Mr Clark was shot through the head shortly after arriving on the island. A machine gun swept the breastwork and got him. He died on the little strip of earth in the early hours of Christmas Day. It seemed to be another case of a life thrown away because a man was tall. Mr Clark was a giant. I can't understand how the military bosses overlooked the shocking handicap which tall men were under in trench warfare. It will never be known how many men lost their lives from wounds received at the six foot mark or above. Surely the artillery was the place for tall chaps, where they were not over-vulnerable by reason of their height. It was bad enough for me at five feet nine and a half to have to keep remembering the height of a parapet.

Our thoughts turned to home and our loved ones on Christmas Day. No letters came; no parcels; nothing. The soggy rations were of the meanest kind, the only pretence at Christmas being a few raisins covered with hairs and other foreign matter from the inside of a sandbag. Stretcher-bearers came after dark for the dead young officer. They had a terrible job carrying him over the duckboards.

It so happened that Jerry was fated to pay a penalty for the officer's death; at least that was the way we chose to look at it. Later that night we became aware of activity in front of the German positions opposite us, where the ground rose slightly. Voices came clearly across No Man's Land, also the sound of hammering. In fact it was the most careless bit of enemy movement in our experience, causing us to wonder whether it was thought that, because it was Christmas night, we would refrain from hostile action. If such was the case, then Jerry made a mistake. Snowy and I reckoned it was a wiring party not more than eighty yards away, and that if we were careful we could bag a good many of them. Leaving the rest of the team on the island, we took the Vickers with muzzle-extension attached and a full belt of ammo. We stealthily worked our way thigh-deep in water until we came to a point fifty yards clear of the island, where we lay on a mound of wet earth. Using a short emergency tripod, Snowy adopted a comfortable firing position close to the ground.

For a few moments we listened to the noise and chatter coming across No Man's Land, which gave us true direction. I fired a Very light into the darkness. Its brilliant white glare clearly revealed the figures of twenty or more Jerries spread out near their wire to a width of thirty yards. The majority of them wore the Kaiser-like spiked helmets. Giving them no time to

disperse, Snowy pressed the trigger of the Vickers, and I fired a
second Very light. The flare burst, casting its glare on the
tottering ghost-like figures as they fell. Swiftly, as if wielding a
two-edged sword, Snowy plied the hail of bullets. Two Jerries
ran into their wire and were trapped. The ground where the
enemy had fallen was raked with fire, to finish off any crafty ones
who might be feigning death. The second flare had just about
burnt itself out as the firing stopped. The whole thing lasted no
more than thirty seconds. In my imagination I can still hear the
sound of the machine gun as it stuttered across the flooded land,
the echoes fading into black silence.

At first there was a deadly quiet after the firing had ceased,
and then came the sound of whistles blowing, cries and
shouting. That was good enough for us. Wading back, we joined
our companions. They had witnessed the slaughter and
unanimously agreed that very few Jerries could have survived.
Enemy activity in front of us continued for some time and we
were tempted to administer another dose. Being reasonably
certain that German stretcher-bearers were at work, we stayed
our hand.

Many years later, an American Jew named Ben Hecht said he
had 'a happy holiday in his heart' every time a British soldier
was killed in Palestine. That about sums up what we felt like
towards Jerry on that Christmas night many years ago. The age-
old sentiment of 'goodwill to all men' meant nothing to us then.
With ten million men under arms on the Western and Eastern
fronts, the expression was invalid. Jerry retaliated with whizz-
bangs and landed one within five yards of our position. This was
close enough in view of the scanty cover of the breastwork.

Our relief came on the fifth night and we plodded back to the
welcome dry warmth of the Béthune tobacco factory. The ten-
kilometre journey in thigh-boots from the island at Festubert
was exhausting. Before I could flop down I had to secure a little
bit of floor space to lie on, scramble for blankets and rations,
remove my mud-encrusted clothing from the waist downwards
revealing the half-pickled skin beneath, deal with irritant lice,
and keep an eye cocked in the direction of my possessions for
fear of swiping—all these jobs and several others had to be done
before I could slip under the blankets into unconsciousness.

After four days' rest and blessed sleep came nine days in the front line at Givenchy, followed by four days' rest in Béthune. Then we went back for five days to Festubert, where we were on the same island as before. Nothing of special significance happened on these spells. The enemy continued to shell the Givenchy and Cuinchy brickfields heavily.

On 18 January 1916 we marched out of the war area to Gonnehem, a drab village five kilometres from Béthune. In fact the whole of the 12th Division was relieved for the first time since the battle of Loos. Number 13 Platoon was billeted in the cosy loft of a barn, full of luxurious hay and straw. Rats ran along the beams and rifled our packs, but we didn't worry. All we wanted was warmth and plenty to eat. It was at Gonnehem that I decided to jettison my souvenirs, weighing nearly twenty pounds, which I had been lugging around in my pack. German fuse tops, funny-shaped bits of shrapnel and a rusty saw-edge bayonet were among this collection of old iron. Why I had been torturing myself with this agonising load I don't know—just a boyish habit of collecting something out of the ordinary, I suppose. 'You're just a bloody twerp carting that lot about,' my pals scoffed. And so, my eyes opened at last, I chucked the stuff away, not without regret, but with substantial relief when the time came to move off.

We had now been in France eight months and had gone through the fires. Christmas was past, and what of the future? To tell the truth, deep down in me I was scared of the future. For the first few months, trench warfare had been a kind of dangerous fun to me. Although only a boy I had lived with grown men, sharing their fears and dangers. It was still fun when not in the trenches. Up in the front line, however, anything approaching merriment was dead. Rude jokes, yes, but no merriment. Everyone has an appetite for amusement and pleasure, the same as for eating. We were starved of the joys and pleasures of life. The dreadful winter, coupled with the constant fear of death and insufficient food, produced a yearning for England and home. I felt that if only I could get leave to see Blighty and know it was really there, I would be able to stick it out.

16 Blighty leave

Rumours circulated about leave, and there was much specu-
lation regarding the method of selection and issue of passes. The
battalion cleaned up and commenced routine chores and
exercises. At the finish of a route march on 14 January, I was
ordered to report to the battalion orderly room. I presented
myself with some trepidation. There I was handed a telegram
from my mother telling me that my step-father had been killed
in France a few days before. He was a sergeant serving in the
East Surreys. A coal-box had dropped in a crowded trench and
had killed him and six of his men. Compassionate leave was
granted me, and I was in a daze when I reported to the railway
transport officer at Chocques late that night. This dramatic turn
in my life bewildered me. I was not at all happy at going home
under such conditions, but, being young, I soon brightened up.
My outstanding regret was that a meeting which my step-father
and I had been trying to arrange never took place.

I arrived in England on my eighteenth birthday, 26 January
1916. It had become the fashion to welcome troops home at
Victoria Station. People pressed forward from the waiting
crowds and gave me packets of cigarettes and chocolate.

Arrival of the leave train at Victoria.   *Imperial War Museum Q30515*

Religious organisations provided lashings of buffet fare and hot drinks. It was just marvellous for a Tommy's homecoming. Leave men carried their rifles, which usually indicated that they had arrived from the front. Most people knew this, and when I went into a pub at East Croydon it never cost me a penny. It was a wonderful thing to feel that people really did care about the Tommies.

Of course, I did not relish seeing my mother a widow, or my little half-sisters and brother fatherless. I visited all my dear relatives, and a happy welcome, they gave me. My uncle A E Coppard, loaned me his motor bike for a couple of days and I remember how cocky I felt, thinking that people imagined I was a dispatch rider.

The wrench came when I had to say goodbye and return to France. Heart-breaking scenes occurred when the troop trains departed. I was in tears. With the companionship of other Tommies, plenty of cigarettes and other good things in my haversack, I soon forgot the tears, especially when I was roped in for a game of Pontoon.

The weather was wild at Folkestone and for two days we hung about waiting. On the third day I boarded the packet-boat. Feeling hungry, I scoffed a couple of pork pies. I joined a Brag school in a warm alleyway alongside the engine room and the game proceeded as the ship moved off in the darkness. She began to roll and plunge as she crossed the bar, with worse to follow, so that even a prial of threes couldn't hold me to the game any longer. The pies erupted violently as I staggered out for air. On arriving back at Gonnehem I struggled hard to adjust to the harsh routine of active service again.

I did not know until after the war that at about this time an uncle of mine, acting on behalf of my mother, wrote to the War Office, pointing out that I was only just eighteen years old and had already 'done my bit' in France for eight months. In view of this he asked for my discharge on the grounds that I was under age, the age for enlistment being nineteen. The War Office replied that their records showed that I was nineteen years old on enlistment and, that being my official age, I could not be released. Apparently the production of my birth certificate cut no ice with them. What a stony-hearted lot they were in those days!

Thos. De La Rue & Co., Ltd., Bunhill Row, E.C.   Form
W3123/1706   1,200m   6/15   C. 349
                                                    61

No. ___G.S.Q./1104\   **MEMORANDUM.**   Army Form C. 348.

From   From
     Colonel i/c Records,

          Hounslow.
To
     Mr B. Watson,   To
          53 Buller Road,

             Brighton.   ANSWER.

          Hounslow.   _____

     12th February ___1916.   _____191

Dear Sir,

          I am in receipt of your letter
dated 6th inst, with reference to No G/701
Pte G.A.Coppard, 6th Battalion The Royal
West Surrey Regiment, being granted his
discharge, and beg to state that as his
age on attestation is 19 years and 7 months,
and that, is therefore his official age,
and it is regretted that your request
for his discharge cannot be acceded to.

          Your's faithfully,

          [signature]
                    Major for Colonel,
     in charge of Records, Hounslow.

Letter from the War Office refusing to discharge the author on grounds of age,
12 February 1916.   *Imperial War Museum Q71269*

17 I am transferred to the Machine Gun Corps

On 5 February 1916 the machine gun section of the 6th Battalion the Queen's was brigaded into the 37th Machine Gun Company of the Machine Gun Corps. We became 'A' Section, probably owing to our regimental seniority. All personnel were issued with new identity discs, my new regimental number being 19012. I had some regrets at losing the Queen's badge with the lamb, but welcomed the new one with two crossed Vickers guns surmounted by the British crown.

There were new faces everywhere, especially among the officers. It was exciting to feel that we were no longer in a small unit, subject to the whims and dictates of every infantry officer and NCO. From then on, as members of a specialised corps, we came under the orders of our own superiors. Carried down the scale, this meant that an unpaid lance-corporal in charge of a gun in action, who became detached from his own superiors, would be the sole judge as to the best position for his gun, and when and where it should be fired.

Our first CO was Captain D K Anderson, a Scot, and a bit of a Tartar to boot. By this I mean that he was dedicated to the task of bringing his new company to a condition of almost brutal efficiency. The standard drill for going into action was complicated, and long and hard practice was needed to get a team into really good shape. On the blow of a whistle, Number One dashed five yards with the tripod, released the ratchet-held front legs so that they swung forward, both pointing outwards, and secured them rigidly by tightening the ratchet handles. Sitting down, he removed two metal pins from the head of the tripod, whereupon Number Two placed the gun in position on the tripod. Number One whipped in the pins and the gun was then ready for loading. Number Three dashed forward with an ammunition box containing a canvas belt, pocketed to hold 250 rounds. Number Two inserted the brass tag-end of the belt into the feed-block on the right-hand side of the gun. Number One grabbed the tag-end and jerked it through, at the same time pulling back the crank handle twice, which completed the loading operation.

For sighting, the flick of a finger sprang the stem of the rear sight into a vertical position. A rapid selection of ranges was provided by a spring-loaded wheel, turned up or down as necessary. Part of the drill when practising on the butts was to knock over steel target plates, and we were expected to do this by accuracy of aim and not by watching the dirt fly as a guide to the target. At Gonnehem we practised for hours, day after day, and gradually improvement came throughout the entire company. Captain Anderson was never satisfied unless our hands were bleeding. The more bits of skin that were knocked off the better he liked it.

Stripping the gun to change a barrel or replace broken parts, and re-assembling it at speed, was a drill of great importance. Several hours were actually spent in doing some of the jobs blindfolded, in order to achieve the utmost familiarity with the various parts of the gun. The different types of stoppage were shown by the position of the crank handle when firing ceased; all gunners were trained to remove the cause of a stoppage in a matter of seconds. Our CO was not a man to give fulsome praise, but he looked pretty satisfied with his new company after ten days' hard work.

The company's new sergeant-major was E S Fuggle, a man of Kent, who came to us from the machine gun section of the 6th Buffs. He was just turned twenty-one and was naturally very keen at that age. We youngsters liked him, for he seemed more intelligent than the majority of CSMs. On 16 February we returned to Béthune and were billeted in empty houses opposite the railway station. There was a tidy air raid on the station, which although trifling compared with Second World War standards, was startling. One bomb dropped in the backyard and blew out all the windows.

18 Return to the Hohenzollern Redoubt

The new company marched to Vermelles and straight into the line, 'A' Section supporting the Queen's in the Hohenzollern Redoubt. It had been arranged that, as far as possible, each section would support its old regiment, a sensible idea which was warmly received. This spell brought a new experience for me, that of officer's batman. I found myself attached to

Lieutenant J Wilkie, a Scot. I wasn't sure what being a batman involved, but it turned out to be a good opportunity to see things from an officer's point of view. Was I recommended for or relegated to the job? I don't know, but I soon found out to my great pleasure that Mr Wilkie regarded me as a comrade, and I grew very attached to him. He was about twenty years old, had a boyish plumpness and wore a tricky little moustache, which I secretly envied. I do believe he was the first Scotsman I had ever met that I came to appreciate and understand, and his brogue was fascinating to listen to. His home was in Sanderstead, near Croydon, which provided something in common between us.

Instead of being stuck in the front line, I shared with Mr Wilkie a half-completed German dugout in a support trench. It had twenty steps leading down to a fair-sized room with hefty timber supports. There was only one entrance, facing the wrong way. The location was well within minnie range, and a hit on the entrance would have been disastrous. With the foulest of luck, a minnie could have pitched straight down the steps. Compared with the lot of my pals in the front line and craters, the dugout was a 'little bit of Heaven'. It was a refuge in between patrols. Mr Wilkie was a very conscientious officer and frequently visited the four guns in his charge; and I was always with him. When on patrol, my role was that of a bodyguard, guide and guarantor of the officer's *bona fides*. It was not unknown for a German with a good knowledge of English to masquerade as a British officer and enter our lines at night. A risky job, but it had been done.

I remember during the Loos battle seeing a very military-looking major complete with monocle and wearing a white collar. He asked me the way to Hay Alley and spoke good English. I never suspected that anything was wrong, though I was puzzled about his collar, as all our officers were then wearing khaki collars. Shortly after there was a scare, and officers dashed about trying to find the gallant major, but he had vanished.

When we were in the dugout I looked after the grub side. Being a domesticated person, I rather enjoyed it. The rations were the same as for the men, but they looked better. We ate together, sang songs and indulged in a game of cribbage occasionally.

On my frequent visits to company HQ I saw the kind of life the officers led when not in the front line or on patrol. They had sleeping-bags and blankets, and room to stretch out for sleep. Batmen were on hand to fetch and carry. Meals and drinks were prepared and placed before them. In addition to rum, whisky was available, a popular brand being Old Orkney or, as the troops called it, 'Officers Only', at 2/6 per bottle. Cartoons and pin-ups decorated the walls, and there was never a lack of the precious weed. Such things, and many other small trifles, demonstrated the great difference between the creature comforts of the officers and the almost complete absence of them for the men. That's what the war was like.

Generally speaking, the gulf between officers and other ranks was a little less marked in the trenches. You could call it a temporary attempt at chumminess. NCOs were more matey by far; but out of the line they resorted to the traditional bullying. Was it nervousness, or merely being toffee-nosed, that made some officers hard to get on with? Few, thank goodness, were sadists. Robert Graves in *Goodbye to All That* says, 'My greatest difficulty was to talk to the men with the necessary air of authority.' I can well believe that remark, as many officers seemed to be troubled with the same thing. The nervousness, strain and irritability of his officers could be responsible for a lot of what Tommy had to put up with. In the final analysis he was always the butt. Robert Graves understood all this, and after he was wounded he said that if he ever went back to France he would 'endeavour to make things easier for the men'.

I must admit that before I met Mr Wilkie I was scared stiff of officers and I believe that at the beginning of the war, and for a good while afterwards, most young soldiers felt the same. As the war progressed this feeling gradually lessened, not because officers were any more friendly but because we youngsters were growing up. We took particular notice of the behaviour of officers under fire and compared our conduct with theirs. All soldiers look for and admire a brave intelligent leader and will even put up with abuse from him providing that at a critical moment he displays courage and leadership.

A heavy fall of snow made patrolling very hard going. The bitter cold made it difficult to keep the guns ready for instant action. Glycerine was added to the water in the cooling jackets to prevent it freezing. Mr Wilkie visited his guns even more frequently in foul weather. One was in a crater, and the periodic relief of the team had to be supervised. On returning to the dugout after a patrol I'd quickly prepare a hot drink of some sort. Although twenty feet down, the blast of minnies often blew out the candle and the trembling earth above would drop in showers on our heads.

We had six days of this, and then five days' rest in Béthune, but the company returned to the same sector again on 6 March. The ferocity of the crater fighting had increased even more, and the 37th Brigade was hard-pressed defending the eight craters that we then held. According to reports, the crater and trench fighters of the brigade were slinging at Jerry an average of 30,000 bombs a day, for three days. The enemy retaliation was equally terrible, and we suffered 3,000 casualties during our fourteen-day spell in that area.

On the night of 18 March the enemy bombarded our lines heavily with gas shells and, in the general confusion that followed, he attacked and captured A and C Craters. Owing to lack of reinforcements, no counter-attack was possible. Our artillery bashed Jerry's neighbouring trenches good and hard, but the newly-captured craters escaped their fire. Gas helmets were worn for three hours and I was nearly suffocated. The helmet was nothing more than a flannel bag soaked in a chemical solution with a piece of mica for a window, which soon steamed up in spite of anti-mist treatment. The primitive mask that was issued when we first arrived in France consisted of a piece of muslin containing a pad of cotton wool. In the event of a gas attack we were told to urinate on the pad and bind it over mouth and nose. During the short time we had these early masks, happily for us, no gas came our way. But if it had, the comical side of the situation would quickly have become tragic for those who couldn't produce. Gas was a devilish weapon, against which those early masks made it impossible to measure one's chances of survival.

'B' Company of the Queen's were the victims of a villainous trick by the Prussians during this spell. Three hundred of them came across No Man's Land feigning surrender, without rifles or equipment, their hands held high, but with pockets full of egg bombs. Just before reaching our wire they flung themselves to the ground and hurled a rain of bombs into 'B' Company's trench, causing many casualties. The blow was so severe that the remnants of the company were unable to put up any strong retaliation. The rest of the battalion was sullen and furious about the trick and called the Prussians bloody bastards. Many vowed some dark revenge when any prisoners were taken. Most Vickers gunners swore a private vendetta. From then on, the advance of a crowd of Jerries with their hands up would be the signal to open fire.

The Berkshires relieved the Queen's on 19 March, and our company marched to Béthune. I grew to love the little town, drab though it was. The estaminets with their cheap wine and feeds of eggs and chips were paradise to us. I had a few extra francs to spend as there was my batman's pay, amounting to a minimum of half a crown per week. Of course, I had to work hard for this. Mr Wilkie's uniform, as well as my own, was stiff with dried mud. It was a good day's work to get the officer's gear all spruced up. However, I managed to escape one or two parades when assisting in the officers' mess, where I waited at table. Listening to the officers' conversation was an intriguing experience, and I was greatly surprised at the deference shown to the CO. Captain Anderson was very much the top man.

Came 28 March, and we were back in that hell hole, the Hohenzollern Redoubt. Mr Wilkie found another German dugout in a support trench called 'Pilgrim's Progress'. We made little progress I'm afraid, though it was mighty lucky for us that the dugout had two entrances. Within half an hour of our taking over, a minnie smacked down, destroying one of the entrances and nearly wrecking the twenty-foot chamber. Mr Wilkie was wounded in the mouth, though not seriously enough to cause him to leave the trenches. Both of us were badly shaken, and it was some while before we got over the dread feeling of what might have happened. The officer produced some rum, and a hefty swig each worked wonders. In fact I think we were just a little bit tight after it.

The bitter cold formed ice on top of the sloppy mud and it was almost impossible to achieve sufficient movement to circulate the blood properly. For men huddled in a few feet of trench or in the craters it must have been murder. The officer and I were lucky in having to patrol the four guns, covering over half a mile to do so, after which we sweated like bulls. Fortunately, winter clothing had been issued, including sleeveless leather jerkins with fur attached, Balaclava caps with ear flaps and lined fingerless gloves. Many cases of trench feet developed. This was a pickling of the skin and flesh caused by the persistent cold and wet, and hospital treatment was a long business. Tins of whale oil were supplied for rubbing into the feet. I rigorously kept up this drill and my feet never bothered me.

Mr Wilkie caught a heavy cold. A sore throat and high temperature followed, and he looked ill. He reported sick, and to my surprise it transpired that he was entitled to his batman while in hospital. An ambulance took us to Chocques, where there was an officers' hospital called Le Château. A brief entry in my diary reads, 'Here we had a lazy time and plenty of good grub.' What more could a young soldier ask for? In eight days Mr Wilkie was fully recovered, but on the way back to Vermelles it was my turn to feel groggy. I had a high temperature and was ordered to go sick. I remember that after a week in hospital at Béthune I failed to get a lift back to Vermelles. Within four hours of leaving the hospital I joined Mr Wilkie in the Hohenzollern Redoubt, and I felt real scared.

The next day was Good Friday. Being an old choir boy of Brighton and Croydon parish churches, my thoughts turned to the Christian significance of that day, and to several three-hour services I had attended in the past on Good Fridays. All that was over and seemed meaningless. My identity disc and paybook said my religion was 'C of E'. To me and most Tommies this meant compulsory church parades on Sundays if the company happened to be well out of the fighting zone. I had a glimpse of an army chaplain now and then, but never anywhere near the trenches. In fact one chaplain had a reputation for being hot stuff at cards and having a strong liking for the bottle. It was no use calling yourself an atheist, as this was considered an old trick to dodge church parade, which, of course, it was. I remember once listening to a talk by the Reverend Studdart Kennedy. He said he went to the front line, and while there a strafe started. A sergeant saw him and said, 'Who are you?' 'I'm the Church,' replied the chaplain. 'Then what the bloody hell are you doing here?' queried the sergeant. The Reverend Kennedy's theme for his talk was, 'There's a time and place for all things, including religion.'

There was only one person I knew whose professed religious beliefs did him any good, and that was a Jew named Levinsky. He came to our company on a draft, and had only been with us for about four weeks when he was given a week's leave in Blighty to attend ceremonies in connexion with the Passover. It is not difficult to imagine the feelings of the Gentiles in the company who had been in France for a year with no leave, or hope of any, in the forseeable future.

On the morning of Easter Sunday the Germans blew up two mines in the redoubt. The blast from one of them knocked Mr Wilkie off his feet. We saw the bulging piecrust slowly rise before the centre burst, hurling the vast mass upwards. In a few moments the descent began and the ground shook with the buffeting. We squirmed to the side of the trench like frightened rabbits. One piece of earth, no more than two ounces in weight, struck the nape of my neck. I had a black-out for a short while, but apart from a stiff neck for a week, I was none the worse for the tap. The Queen's lost men that Easter morning from the two explosions, which destroyed the front line where they were standing. Jerry made no attempt to capture the craters.[1]

19 The 12th Division rests

Relief came on 25 May and we marched back to Vermelles brewery for the night. Next day we entrained from Noeux-les-Mines to Lillers. Some top brass must have taken pity on us after what we had been through. Our journey ended in the pleasant village of Allouagne, five kilometres from Lillers. Mr Wilkie was billeted in a comfortable room in a farmhouse, while I had quarters in a little bakehouse at the top end of the farmyard. 'A' Section occupied a cosy barn on another side of

---

[1] In a recent quarterly news letter of the Machine Gun Corps Old Comrades Association, there was an item from a member who was at the Hohenzollern Redoubt in 1918. He says: 'I had my moments in the Redoubt in 1918. I think it was 9th October when the rumour went along the line, "JERRY IS GONE". It was true. We were ordered to pack up and move forward to where Hulluch once stood. The end of the Redoubt, bitterly known to Mr Coppard and thousands of others, was as simple as that.' The fighting in the redoubt lasted over three years, with very little movement.

the yard, which was full of sweet-smelling manure. Cattle and poultry scratched and lazed around. Watching them was a simple pleasure, the very essence of peace and tranquillity.

Named Bailleul, the farmer and his wife were typical French peasants, and had two teenage daughters, Marie and Maria. The family were very kind and frequently invited me to supper, though I wasn't keen on the cabbage soup which they seemed to have every night. Maria would often give me a whacking great slice of bread of her own making, liberally spread with fresh salted butter, which I helped to produce. Milk was poured into a barrel which had a rod through the centre, resting on bearings. I sat and oscillated the barrel by pulling a cord, while Maria darned Mr Wilkie's socks. It was a great pity I couldn't speak French, but the eyes played their part, and I was quite happy just to sit and look at Maria without speaking.

For several days I was employed in the officers' mess. When the officers were out I improved my musical education on their gramophone. Mendelssohn's Midsummer Night's Dream was my favourite, and his Spring Song and Wedding March tied for second place. A very good third was Melody in F by Rubinstein. I loved that gramophone. One Sunday, to the toll of the village church bell, numbers of angelic-looking children, dressed in white, hurried along to be confirmed by the bishop. It was a pretty sight, but somehow a little perplexing, for there was I, not very much older than some of the children, caught up in the blood and thunder of a ghastly war.

The weather was good, and all units in the division were engaged in training of some sort. Then came big schemes of manoeuvring and mock battles. Staff officers, red-tabbed and beribboned, dashed all over the place with immense bravado, giving their orders and comments in cracking military style. I certainly admired them for their immaculate appearance. Most Tommies looked such a scruffy crowd by comparison. One thing was certain, and that was the near approach of an offensive against the enemy.

Company sports took place and I picked up two francs as second prize in the batman's race. I knew next to nothing about horses or mules, but allowed myself to be kidded into competing in the mule race. My mount, named Norman, was generally regarded as the most recalcitrant of the stubborn bunch who pulled our limbers. The distance was a quarter of a mile, and the course ran alongside a field of corn. Norman shot ahead and cunningly suggested that I was on my way to an easy victory, but he veered sharply and deliberately bucked me off. So ended my first and only mule ride.

In the evenings there were Housey-Housey sessions outside an estaminet in the middle of the village, with crowds of Tommies sitting on the ground knocking back wine and beer. The game—called Bingo today—was the only game of chance allowed in the army then. Those in the mood for more serious gambling games, such as Crown and Anchor, Banker or Pontoon, slunk off to lonely spots, away from the vigilance of the military police. Some of the French paper money which we used for gambling was issued by the Chambers of Commerce of various towns—Amiens, Arras and so on. The notes were of small value, from half a franc to two francs. I was curious about the facsimile signature of the cashier on one of the notes. It was Edouard Coppard. There are a few Coppards in Sussex, and as I first saw the light of day in that county I wondered whether Edouard was very distantly related to me, way back in 1066. At the end of a Housey session the top dogs running it threw away the dirty notes of small value. A rough house in the dirt was a sight worth watching as Tommies fought for the notes.

One fine evening, with a big crowd all set for a game, two military policemen appeared with a handcuffed prisoner and, in full view of the crowd and villagers, tied him to the wheel of a limber, cruciform fashion. The poor devil, a British Tommy, was undergoing Field Punishment Number One, and this public exposure was a part of the punishment. There was a dramatic silence as every eye watched the man being fastened to the wheel, and some jeering started. Scenting trouble, the Housey-Housey king shouted out, 'Eyes down! Look in! Kelly's eye! Harry Tate!' and the game got under way. An hour passed and suddenly a scuffle started, with a couple of Tommies rolling on the ground and making a great show of pummelling each other. The military policemen ran over to separate them, but the two frolickers assured them that the scramble was just a friendly caper. In the meantime the prisoner had gulped down several swigs from a bottle of wine neatly produced by other conspirators. Lashing men to a wheel in public in a foreign country was one of the most disgraceful things in the war. The troops resented these exhibitions, but they continued until 1917, when the War Minister put a stop to them following protests in Parliament.

I believe that an important modification of the death sentence also took place in 1917. It appeared that the military authorities were compelled to take heed of the clamour against the death sentences imposed by courts martial. There had been too many of them. As a result, a man who would otherwise have been executed was instead compelled to take part in the forefront of the first available raid or assault on the enemy. He was purposely placed in the first wave to cross No Man's Land and it was left to the Almighty to decide his fate. This was the situation as we Tommies understood it, but nothing official reached our ears. I have no knowledge whether a prisoner surviving an attack on the enemy had expiated his offence by deliberate exposure to the will of Providence. Let the War Office dig out its musty files and tell us how many men were treated in this way, and how many survived the cruel sentences. Shylock, in demanding his pound of flesh, had got nothing on the military bigwigs in 1917.

Historians say that Haig had the confidence of his men. I very much doubt whether this was strictly true. He had such a vast number of troops under his command and was so completely remote from the actual fighting that he was merely a name, a figurehead. In my view, it was not confidence in him that the men had, but simply their ingrained sense of duty and obedience, in keeping with the times. They were wholly loyal to their own officers, and that was as far as their confidence went. It was trust and comradeship founded on the actual sharing of dangers together.

Divisional training continued well into June. Lord Kitchener had just been drowned at sea when travelling to Russia on board HMS *Hampshire*—a strange end for a field-marshal. We were puzzled by this unfortunate event, and genuinely sorry for him, as well as for the poor sailors who lost their lives. We will never know whether it would have made any difference had he reached Russia, but at the time Kitchener's death seemed an ill omen.

On the night of 14 June, in conjunction with the French, we advanced our time in accordance with the Daylight Saving Act. Two days later we left Allouagne. I was sorry to say farewell to the Bailleul family, especially Maria. She wrote me one letter I could hardly read, and that was the end.

The company marched to Lillers and entrained for Amiens. It was strange passing through the city, with big solid buildings on either side of the streets. The shops were open and the market place was packed. One of the officers had returned from leave with four mouth organs, and 'Tipperary' was in full swing as we marched past the great cathedral. Women and children waved flags and cheered as the column moved on. We slogged along on the hot cobbled stones for eighteen kilometres, which brought us to Naours, a lonely unlovely village. Nobody had any money except a few coppers. In the dull evenings we played 'Penny up the line'. To brighten our lives, the Queen's fife and drum band regaled us with a few martial airs before retreat. One of the tunes was the regimental march, and the traditional words, 'Here they come, here they come, bloody great bastards every one', seemed appropriate to a crowd of troops with very little money.

There were supposed to be some famous subterranean caves near the village, but few of us were interested in such a dull subject. Being without money was a pretty painful ordeal. We had some pay due to us, but got nothing. This occurred many times. Hundreds of men mouching around in a dreary village without the price of a drink is an unhappy sight. The officers with their duty-free whisky would be having a riotous booze-up in the best house in the village, and we poor blighters would be fuming and cursing. The carousing officers' sing-song would echo long into the night. 'There's One Green Bottle Hanging on the Wall', and 'Old Macdonald had a Farm', were two of their popular numbers, invariably accompanied by rhythmic thumping. Out of pure envy, we'd work up a counter-rumpus in nearby billets by banging on tin cans and shouting and whistling, until silenced by some awful threat from the orderly sergeant. I don't blame the officers for having a booze-up, but the men expected their pay on the dot or there was trouble. My saddest memory of the war is my continual state of poverty.

20 The Somme battle

On 27 June the company left Naours and marched to St Gratien, which was on the road to Albert. Steel helmets had been issued, and with the extra weight and bulk we didn't much care for them. The time came when I couldn't bear the thought of being without my helmet. Our rifles had been handed in and revolvers issued in lieu, but we retained our bayonets. I had a Colt .45 — quite a weapon. Revolver handling had been part of our recent training and we had had a good deal of target practice. There is no doubt that we were by that time extremely efficient machine gunners, and we were going into the Somme battle with confidence in our officers and in our ability to get the best possible results from our Vickers gun. With a year's actual fighting experience behind us, and our intensive training, we knew what to do and how to do it. The parts which we each and severally were to play were in the hands of Fate. The bulk of the company were men of Surrey and Kent, good solid stock. So far as I know there were no poets or writers among us. We were merely the raw material to inspire the lofty musings of others. And so, on we went, singing the bawdy songs we loved so well, towards one of the greatest, most terrible and frustrating battles in history. 'Today's my daughter's wedding day. Twenty thousand pounds I'll give away. Hooray! Hooray! . . .'

The joint Anglo-French attack was designed to relieve heavy German pressure on Verdun in the south. According to the special commemorative issues of the French magazine *Paris Match* in August 1964, 26 divisions were British and 14 were French, and the total territory gained during the whole of the Somme battle was about eighty square kilometres. The salient of captured land was thirty-nine kilometres in width, with a maximum depth of eight kilometres; roughly seven miles square all told. For this miserable fraction of the earth's surface. approximately three-quarters of a million British and French soldiers became casualties. The reference books state that the battle lasted from 1 July to 20 November, and that the total British loss was 22,293 officers and 476,553 NCOs and men. Judging from the articles in *Paris Match*, written fifty years after the great battle, the pressure on Verdun was not greatly reduced. If this is true, then a stalemate is the best that can be said for the Somme offensive, but a points win for Jerry seems nearer the truth.

On the night of 30 June the 37th Machine Gun Company rested in a field near Albert. A fierce bombardment of the German lines was going on. We were in the area of the big guns of 9.2-inch calibre. They were underneath camouflage nets and looked huge, bigger than anything we'd seen before, Six-inch Long Toms—a naval gun adapted for land use, I believe—were belching flames, while the 4.7-inch howitzers nearer the front lines swelled the colossal roar.

On the afternoon of 1 July, a date that will never be forgotten, we passed through Albert on our way to the front. We knew that the great assault had started early that morning. The red-brick cathedral looked in a sorry state. Adding to its wrecked appearance was the massive golden figure of the Virgin on the tall tower, leaning over at an angle of about 95 degrees. At first we thought that crack shooting by Jerry artillery had knocked the figure over, but later on we learned that French engineers had bent it down to prevent the enemy from using its great height as an artillery fix.

There was a terrific crowd of troops and vehicles at Crucifix Corner. The road forked there and in the angle, commanding the approach, stood a huge crucifix. The sorrowful face of Christ gazed down at the turmoil below. I remember looking at His face—a glance only—there was no time for more. Many men, who had passed by on their way to the front not many hours before, were now dead; and many more were to follow them. The left fork led to Thiepval, la Boisselle and Ovillers. The right led to Fricourt and Contalmaison. We took the left fork, glad to get away from the congestion. The thunder of the guns and the scream of shells passing close above us were nerve-racking. We were also exposed to premature bursts from the field guns close behind us, and we needed no urging to speed up our steps. It must have been torture for the horses and mules to have to stand still when masses of stores and ammo were being unloaded. Every two or three minutes a salvo of coal-boxes crashed in the area, bringing wholesale death and destruction.

I should mention here that I was now back as Number Two in Snowy Hankin's gun team. Being a batman had its good points but somehow I felt less than a complete soldier, for though there

Albert: the Leaning Virgin, 1917. The gilded statue of the Virgin and Child
which surmounted the church was knocked sideways by a German shell
early in 1915. It was a popular belief in the British army that its fall would
signify the end of the war. The statue was maintained in its precarious
position by the Royal Engineers and thousands of British troops gazed up at
it as they passed through Albert on their way to the Somme. After the
British withdrawal from Albert in March 1918 the church tower was
demolished to prevent its use by the Germans as an observation post. The
statue was never found.   *Imperial War Museum CO 2132*

was almost as much danger in the job there was certainly more personal comfort. I was content to be back in the team. The little pin-pricks they had occasionally dished out about my having a cushy job ceased. The other four members of the team were Marshall, Armstrong, Curly Barnes and Nobby Clark.

We moved ahead over rising ground with the Vickers and equipment, thankful that we no longer had to carry a rifle and 120 rounds of ammo. Climbing Coniston Steps, which were cut into a steep bank, we entered Aveluy Wood. Jerry was shelling it heavily with dirty black shrapnel shells, nicknamed 'Woolly Bears', having rightly guessed that the wood was packed with troops. The powerful crump of these shells as they burst at tree-top level was frightening.

To make things even more unpleasant, lachrymatory or tear shells literally drenched the wood. They caught us unawares, stinging the eyes painfully; tears poured down our faces as we staggered about like blind men. It was too late to put on gas masks. We tried them but they had no effect. The noxious liquid hung about, and it was not until we were clear of the wood that we got any relief. The thick reek of smoke from explosives and tear gas clung to the foliage like fumes from a devil's cauldron, nearly shutting out the bright sky above. A winding track led through the wood, and many wounded and dying men lay on either side of it, but we could not stay to help them. A steady stream of walking wounded were making their way down to Coniston Steps, and away out of it all. I envied those who did not appear to be seriously hit. One could hardly bear thinking about the agony of the badly wounded who lay unattended.

Clear of the wood at last, we climbed into a trench, and before nightfall mounted the Vickers. The name given to that part of the front was la Boisselle, a village just behind the German lines. As far as we could gather, the attack that morning had started at 7.30 am from the trench in which we stood. Darkness fell before we could sum up the situation in No Man's Land, but the number of our dead in front of the gun position was an ominous clue.

Our primary job was defence, but we put up long bursts of indirect fire throughout the night, harassing the support areas immediately behind the enemy trenches. Our firing was unwelcome and attracted a steady search by a Jerry whizz-bang battery. We brought in a number of wounded men who had fallen near our trench and bandaged them up. They told us how the enemy had been picking off the wounded as they lay in shell holes under the hot sun. As we were under the eye of the Germans any properly organised rescue work was ruled out, and the wounded had mostly to tend and help each other. With a British casualty figure of 60,000 on the first day of the struggle, it was beyond the power of man to give aid except to a few. Many were out there in front of us, and their cries for help continued for days. Those who were able to crawl lived on the water and rations they could find on their dead comrades. By day, under the boiling sun, they had to lie motionless in shell holes and depressions, for fear of being finished off. At night, German patrol parties were out on the prowl, and clashes occurred with British patrols making attempts at rescue work. Only a wounded man who had spent days in such a trap could really describe what it was like. I thank Providence that I was not one of them.

21 'I've seen 'em, I've seen 'em, hanging on the old barbed wire'

The next morning we gunners surveyed the dreadful scene in front of our trench. There was a pair of binoculars in the kit, and, under the brazen light of a hot mid-summer's day, everything revealed itself stark and clear. The terrain was rather like the Sussex downlands, with gentle swelling hills, folds and valleys, making it difficult at first to pinpoint all the enemy trenches as they curled and twisted on the slopes. It soon became clear that the German line followed points of eminence, always giving a commanding view of No Man's Land. Immediately in front, and spreading left and right until hidden from sight, was clear evidence that the attack had been brutally repulsed. Hundreds of dead, many belonging to the 37th Brigade, were strung out like wreckage washed up to a high-water mark. Quite as many had died on the enemy wire as on the ground, like fish caught in a net. They hung there in grotesque postures. Some looked as though they were praying: they had died on their knees and the wire had prevented their fall.

From the way the bodies were evenly spread out, whether on

the wire or lying in front of it, it was clear that there were no gaps in the wire at the time of the attack. Concentrated machine-gun fire from sufficient guns to command every inch of the wire had done its terrible work. The Germans must have been reinforcing their wire for months. It was so dense that daylight could barely be seen through it. Through the glasses it looked almost solid. The German faith in massed wire had paid off.

How did our planners imagine that Tommies, having survived all the other hazards—and there were plenty in crossing No Man's Land—would break through the German wire? Had they studied the black density of it through their powerful binoculars? What made them think that artillery fire would pound such wire to pieces? Any Tommy could have told them that shell-fire lifts wire up and drops it down, often in a worse tangle than before. A vast amount of our artillery fire was directed against the enemy wire before 1 July, but with the huge percentage of misses it was largely wasted effort. Brave men of the Royal Engineers went out at night before the assault to explode torpedoes under the wire, but it flopped back.

In my opinion the German troops were in no way superior to the British. What was superior beyond any doubt was the enemy trench system, built in thorough German fashion to a proper standard of strength and efficiency, and defended with large numbers of machine guns. It was the strength of this system that was seriously under-estimated. The morale of the German troops behind such defences was bound to be high, as there was every likelihood that they would be able to beat off an attack. Any talk of the lack of experience of our troops is a cruel slander. If every one of our boys had been a highly-trained Guardsman, he could have done no more than reach the wire—if he got as far as that—and then die. The very manner of their death is proof that our assault troops on those first terrible days hadn't a dog's chance. What I saw on the morning of 2 July convinced me that our chaps had been totally unable to get to grips with Jerry. The reason was simple enough. Someone had blundered about the wire. Any element of initiative or surprise had already been ruined by the long bombardment of the enemy trenches, commencing as far back as 2 June. Jerry thus had ample time to repair and strengthen his defences, and lay doggo in deep dugouts waiting for us.

There are still things to tell of the battle and I must return to it. On 2 July Jerry opened a prolonged shelling of our sector and one of 'A' Section's guns was blown up, two of the team being badly wounded. On the same day Snowy and I had a narrow squeak when a coal-box landed between the front legs of the gun-tripod, but failed to explode. Although it was flung into the air, the gun wasn't damaged. The unerring convergence of sound bearing down on the spot where we stood gave us a split-second warning, and we threw ourselves on the ground. Thank heavens the shell was a dud. We hastily constructed a new emplacement for the Vickers some distance away. The enemy shelling continued very close to our trench, and we took possession of an unoccupied dugout. Dangerous though it was with only one entrance, we couldn't resist the shelter its overhead cover gave us. The risk was there, and we gambled that nothing would happen; but a coal-box struck the top of the dugout and the timber supports below collapsed on three of the team. Two were dug free quickly, but Snowy, who had been stretched out, was pinned down by earth and corrugated iron, with just his face clear. Loose earth kept dropping as shells shook the ground; in the dim and fast-fading light of an electric torch it took two hours to free him. Trapped and helpless though he was, Snowy was joking most of the time, and offering advice as to the best way to dig him out. He did not panic or become excited, and calmly waited while we worked. An officer was present, and witnessed this example of cool courage. Sometime later Snowy was awarded the Military Medal, the first in the 37th Machine Gun Company.

On 3 July the Queen's and the Royal West Kents attacked the German lines from our sector. Crossing the corpse-strewn No Man's Land towards the black enemy wire, draped with dead Tommies, they met fierce machine-gun fire, and were completely repulsed. Many walking wounded who managed to struggle back filtered down our trench towards Aveluy Wood. I remember one youngster asking me to bandage him up. His right wrist had been lacerated by a large piece of shrapnel and the hand was hanging by a few sinews. The initial shock must have stifled the pain and he was almost cheery. 'I've got a Blighty at last,' he said. Like all of us, his desire to get out of it all and live was so strong that the loss of his hand was of secondary importance.

I bandaged another chap whose arm, when in a horizontal position, had been hit by a bullet which shattered the whole forearm from wrist to elbow. The flesh was literally hanging in tatters. My first-aid effort, I'm afraid, was nothing more than parcelling up the pieces. The terrible injury caused by this one bullet made us wonder if Jerry was using dum-dum bullets. Later on, we found several clips of German soft-nosed bullets, and, as opportunity offered, experienced grim satisfaction in shooting them back with Mauser rifles. Such action was probably against international convention, but we knew nothing about such things. We did know that Jerry was using saw-edge bayonets, flame-throwers and poison gas when it suited him. Simple justice demanded that whatever he used against us it was meet and proper for him to get back.

News spread that Contalmaison, a village about five kilometres south, had been captured. None of us went into raptures over this information, as the 12th Division had not yet made a breach in the enemy line. All praise to the troops who captured the village, but what is a village in a battle area? A pile of bricks and rubble, with a fearful stench of death—not much to show for the terrible price paid.

The weather continued very hot. In fact it was a glorious summer that year. Water was severely rationed. Gruesome and distasteful though it was, we augmented our supplies from the dead. Looking at it today, it seems pretty low-down to plunder dead men's belongings, but needs must, and we soon got over the guilty feeling. A tin of bully in a dead man's pack can't help him, nor can a packet of cigarettes. Many a good smoke came our way in this manner. In spite of our fears and privations life was still sweet provided we had a smoke.

Relief came on 9 July. Once we were clear of Aveluy Wood and down Coniston Steps our spirits rose. Exhausted, filthy and crawling with lice, we tramped through Albert and beyond to a village called Warloy. The order to polish buttons and brass as well as boots set off a spate of the foulest language. We felt tricked over the polishing business, not being in the mood for calculated goading of that kind. Jerry had given us all the goading we wanted. Yet, there it was, it had to be done, and the Lord help those who didn't do it properly. And so we swore like hell and polished our buttons. At Vauchelles-les-Authie General Scott inspected our company and congratulated us on our behaviour in the trenches. By way of a change, it would have been appropriate if he had seen us at the time of leaving the line, instead of through the rosy-tinted glasses of spit and polish. But generals don't work that way.

Twice during the ten days we were alerted and marched back to Albert in preparation for a return to the line, but the alarms subsided and we finished our rest. The great battle was still raging, and small gains were made at various points. On 25 July we took over trenches near Ovillers, which had just been captured by the Australians. We mounted the Vickers in the old German front line of 1 July, the exact sector that we had faced from our position in front of Aveluy Wood. Our dead were still hanging on the wire, but were shortly removed and buried.

It was staggering to see the high standard of the trenches that the Jerry front-line troops had used. We envied the skill and industry employed in constructing such comfortable yet powerful defences. Some of the dugouts were thirty feet deep, with as many as sixteen bunk-beds, as well as door bells, water tanks with taps, and cupboards and mirrors. Apart from the personal comfort enjoyed by the Germans in them, the deep dugouts had withstood everything that our heavy artillery had flung at them. When our hearts had leapt at the seemingly devastating bombardment of those trenches, and had imagined that Jerries were being smashed to bits, the enemy were in all probability playing cards or carousing. In the dugout we occupied we found several packs of cards, and every corner was full of empty wine and beer bottles. Leaving aside such things as personal courage and endurance, it seemed as if we were a load of amateurs when compared with the professional thoroughness of the Germans. It certainly wasn't the fault of the British Tommy that he didn't have decent dugouts. If he had been given the materials and proper instruction, not only would he have enjoyed greater comfort, but thousands of lives would have been saved.

The whole conduct of our trench warfare seemed to be based on the concept that we, the British, were not stopping in the trenches for long, but were tarrying awhile on the way to Berlin and that very soon we would be chasing Jerry across country.

The result, in the long term, meant that we led a mean and impoverished sort of existence in lousy scratch holes.

In the early days of August, things were a little quieter in the la Boisselle–Ovillers area. After a month of bitter fighting both sides were consolidating their position. I was a Number One gunner then and Nobby Clark was my Number Two. Nobby was a good deal older than I was, thirty perhaps, steadfast and very strong. I was conscious of my new responsibility and felt gratified that I had been picked for the job. It was up to me to put all I knew into keeping the Vickers in fighting trim.

The weather was still fine, and there were magic moments during quiet spells when grub was cooking on a fire and someone vamped on a mouth organ. We'd lift our voices and go through the whole of our repertoire, which usually included the following:

> There was once a gay Cavallero,
> Who dwelt on the banks of Navero,
> Flashing about with his wonderful,
> Wonderful, to-ra-la, to-ra-li-ay.

Many bawdy verses follow, and describe the sticky end of that gallant gentleman.

It is appropriate to mention here that the telling of risqué stories was an important feature of trench life. Scores of them were always current and our ears were cocked ready to pick up the latest one going around. They were the one thing that brought a sparkle into our lives, if only for a moment or two, making us forget our trials and troubles. The manner of the telling was crucial, the quiet confidential technique being the one most often employed. A fellow would approach you with a serious air, take hold of your elbow and edge you away from the others, as if to make a personal and private disclosure. You guessed that a yarn was coming but pretended ignorance. He would lead by saying, 'Have you heard the one about so and so?' If the reply was in the negative then all was well and you waited in high anticipation for the moment when you were supposed to fall over in a paroxysm of laughter. As a story travelled so it became garbled, embroidered or stretched to the point of longwindedness; but so long as the final burst of laughter hit you it was considered a winner and you dashed off to try it on some other bloke.

A popular joke that spread like wildfire told of the cockney soldier who was about to enter a dugout in a newly captured German trench. With a Mills bomb in his hand he shouted down the dugout steps, 'Anybody there?' Back came the answer, 'Nein.' 'Nine, eh? Well bloody well share that amongst yer,' and he hurled the bomb down the steps.

Revolver practice was a favourite pastime if there was any spare ammo about. A rifle cartridge pressed deep into a sandbag until just the rim was visible made a target as big as a sixpence. You stood thirty feet back with revolver cocked. If you made a hit, you blew a nice-sized hole in the sandbag, and raised a cheer. Three hits out of five shots was considered good. An enjoyable prank of Snowy's and mine was testing the resistance of the steel helmets that lay scattered about by wielding a pick and bringing it down with all one's might. Snowy, with his forestry-trained biceps, was pretty expert at it. A sound British helmet yielded only a moderate dent, but a dud would burst open down to the shaft of the pick handle. We couldn't very well experiment on our own helmets, in case they should turn out to be duds. Clearly, some cunning war contractor had been cheating and a War Office check hadn't been properly carried out. The duds were obviously of little use against shrapnel, and it is reasonable to assume that men had lost their lives wearing them. Our crude testing proved that German helmets were less resistant than ours, as we could always knock a hole in them. Collecting military badges from the dead was indulged in by many Tommies. I wore a broad leather belt that was covered with them, and I regret that I parted with it for five francs. Today, such a belt might fetch a tidy sum in a London sale room.

Ghoulish curiosity drove me to turn over Jerry corpses for souvenirs, and I acquired a couple of watches and a Luger pistol. One of the watches had a natty bell alarm, something quite new to us. It came in useful for ringing the night hours to mark the changing of the gun reliefs. Searching for souvenirs when things were quiet was rather like looking for mushrooms. You could explore for hours without success and then suddenly strike it lucky. It could be rewarding to pick up a Luger pistol or a pair of German binoculars, as there was always someone who wanted to buy, but there was no organised buying or selling. Pickelhaubes were favourite souvenirs as the mere display of one of these

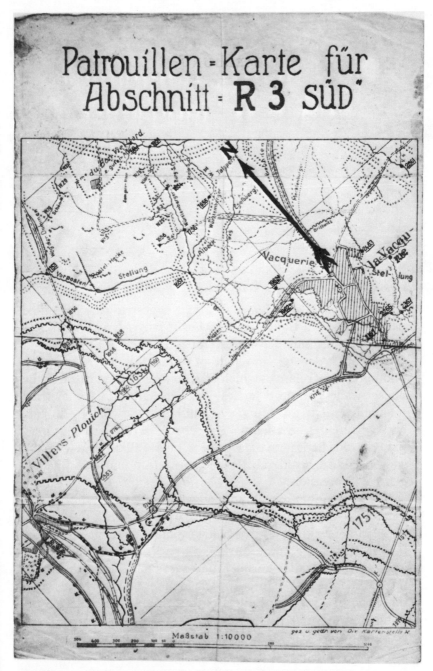

Patrol map of the la Vacquerie sector found by the author on a dead
German.   *Imperial War Museum Q71270*

when you were on leave sort of suggested that you had personally killed the original owner. Many Mauser rifles and other weapons must have been smuggled back to England.

I must say I felt a touch of sympathy when scanning photographs of relatives which I found when I went through the pocket wallets on dead Jerries. They looked ordinary civilised human beings to my young eyes, although they belonged, part and parcel, to the enemy. There were wives and children, parents, old chaps with big whiskers, nearly all dressed in black, as if attending a funeral. Respectable, clean and tidy was the general impression.

But I remember one photo that gave me a bit of a shock. The picture showed a row of a dozen Jerry soldiers with their backs to the camera, sitting on a long latrine pole above a pit. Each man had his shirt pulled up, exposing his backside and genitals. All wore big grins as they looked round over their shoulders and, as if to crown the ugly sight, the pickelhaubes on their heads gave them the appearance of a leering bunch of devils engaged on some hellish prank. I gazed at the corpse beside me and, recognising that it bore a strong resemblance to one of the group, I wondered what had happened to the rest. If that was typical German humour, then, war or no war, Tommies were a lot of angels by comparison, I thought. As one of my pals, a man

View of the battlefield at Thiepval, September 1916. Thiepval, a key point in the German defences, was one of the British army's objectives on the first day of the battle of the Somme. It was taken after 89 days of savage fighting, which reduced the village to a mass of rubble. It was not rebuilt after the war. Thiepval Memorial records the names of over 70,000 officers and men who were killed during the Somme offensive and who have no known grave.   *Imperial War Museum Q1073*

of few words, said, 'There's no doubt about it, they're a dirty lot of bastards.'

On 12 August my team was told off for barrage fire, to assist the Aussies' attack on Thiepval. The position of my gun would enable its fire to enfilade the ground between the new German front line and support trenches, at a point where the attack was to be made that night. As sixteen thousand rounds had to be fired, the team were kept busy fetching ammo and generally making ready. Clinometer calculations were made by an officer, and at early dusk Nobby and I crept out to a shell hole at the back of the parados and mounted the gun, to which we had fitted a new barrel.

It was quiet just before zero and then, suddenly, the sky was ablaze, as if by continuous flash-lightning. The thunderous roar of our artillery reached us on the instant as the screaming shells sped towards the target. The bombardment blasted Jerry's front line and later developed into a creeping barrage on his support trenches. At zero plus fifteen minutes I opened fire and, with the aid of a shaded light and two pre-set pegs, kept the gun in its correct elevation and scope of traverse. I whipped through the first belt in less than half a minute. I then reloaded, gave the gun a check-up and continued the process. In the meantime, Number Three was crawling to and fro, building up the supply of ammo. The rest of the team were in the dugout, filling the empty belts by a hand-operated machine. Periodically, fresh water was added to the cooling jacket, and a touch of oil was applied to the sensitive parts of the gun with a brush kept in one of the grip handles. Although it was dark, we could see and feel what we were doing without difficulty. The ammo, British cordite type, gave little trouble. Now and then a stoppage occurred, but the position of the crank handle quickly indicated the action needed to clear it. Things were going nicely; the bombardment had eased off and I wondered how the attack had fared. I knew there was a chance of success, as Jerry, already driven from the powerful front line, now had to fight in weaker support trenches behind flimsy wire.

Various signal flares lit the sky but were of no significance to us, as our firing had to continue until stand-to. Our job was to assist in pinning the enemy down in his support trenches, and to harass any reinforcements coming forward. We had been told that a sunken road was likely to be used, which also had to receive our attention. I kept up the fire, and, as we had expected, a whizz-bang battery began to search for us. Clark and I were apprehensive, although not exactly displeased, as we guessed our fire must be having some effect. If the German infantry asked for assistance from their light artillery, it was on the cards we were causing mischief. The first whizz-bang landed about twenty yards to the right. The range was bang-on, and a little adjustment in direction was all Jerry needed. The shells came nearer, some a few yards to the left. One hit two yards in front, showering us with dirt and fumes. It looked as if any minute time would stop so far as we were concerned. My stomach rolled in a funk, and I know Clark felt the same. Keeping the gun going was the surest antidote to our rising fears, and that we did. Nobody came and said, 'Pack it up', so we stuck it out and carried on. We finished our quota of rounds in four and a half hours, so our firing was more or less continuous.

Whizz-bangs were a torment to us. They travelled faster than

sound. If you happened to be near the receiving end, you first
heard the thing burst, then the whizz of its approach and lastly
the boom of the gun that fired it. There was no split-second
warning to get one's self-preservation instincts to work, as was
the case with howitzer shells, which had higher trajectories and
less speed.

At dusk one evening Marshall and I were standing close
together talking when a whizz-bang arrived without warning.
There was a powerful plonk, some smoke and a shower of dirt
which covered us, then all was quiet. We were well and truly
shaken. It was clear that the dud missile had actually passed,
chest high, between our bodies, which had only been two feet
apart. It was a very narrow squeak indeed. The following
morning we peered down the hole in the parados to see if the
shell was visible and gingerly poked the end of it with a stick.

I must mention here that Captain Graves in *Goodbye to All
That* refers to machine gun crews indiscriminately firing off
belt after belt to boil their water. This suggests that machine
gunners who fancied a cup of tea or a shave simply loosed off a
couple of belts. In fact, this was not the case, as tea laced with
mineral oil would taste pretty ghastly. Also machine-gun crews
who seemed to be firing 'indiscriminately' might well be
engaged on barrage fire, and infantry officers would not
necessarily be aware of that fact.

Captain Anderson told my team that the Australian GOC had
sent a 'Thank you very much' telegram for our work in assisting
his men on the night of 12 August. It was a most encouraging
message for us. Bearing in mind that the general would get his
knowledge first hand from his own troops, it proved that
although we could not actually see our target we had taken an
effective part in the attack. Relief came on 13 August, and that
night the company bivouaced in a field near Albert. A storm
arose and we were washed out, water running over us as we lay
on ground sheets. It was rumoured that the King would review
the 37th Brigade, but he must have been told of the soaking and
the review was put off.

We marched through Léavillers, Bus and Halloy by easy
stages, and on 17 August we fetched up at Grand Rullecourt.
General Scott presented medal ribbons to a number of officers
and men, and Snowy Hankin got his Military Medal. Captain

Anderson and Lieutenant Hudson received their Military Cross ribbons. The latter officer was a very daring man, dedicating himself to all sorts of private schemes for strafing Jerry. At night, he spent most of his time prowling about in No Man's Land. On one occasion he wanted to take a Vickers and three men on a raid with their pockets loaded with Mills bombs. How they were to get the gun into action, and for what purpose, was never made clear. The scheme wasn't approved. I'm sure Mr Hudson was disappointed, as he was such a restless man of action. But he took too many risks, and none of us was surprised when he was killed shortly afterwards.

The company moved to Arras and slept in the vaults honeycombed beneath the town. The old Spanish-looking façade of the square was in a mess, and the cathedral was a pile of rubble. The square, or Barbed Wire Square as the troops called it, was indeed a mass of wire and shell holes. The town hall at one end of the square was a shambles.[1]

22 'Whizz-bang Villa'

The company took over machine gun posts on 21 August near Rivière, ten kilometres south-west of Arras and opposite Blairville, which hugged the German front line. Snowy's gun and mine were near each other, on the edge of an orchard about a hundred yards from Jerry. To our pleasant surprise, a number of fruit trees were still standing and bearing fruit, but they were in full view of the enemy. Damsons, plums and apples tempted us, as well as a few cordon pears. Our mouths watered at the thought of getting some of the fruit, but how? It had to be done in darkness, as daylight scrumping was out. Jerry no doubt read our minds, and like a son-of-a-bitch belted through the trees as soon as it was dark, repeating the dose every half hour. Like the fox after the grapes, the fruit worried us. The machine-gun fire eased off about 2 am, and we quietly got busy. We gorged like school kids, having almost forgotten what fresh fruit tasted like.

---

[1] In 1958, the touring bus stopped at Arras and the driver gave me ten minutes to find the square. I found a masterpiece of French restoration work. Everything was comparatively new, and yet bore the stamp of age, looking as if peace had reigned there since medieval times.

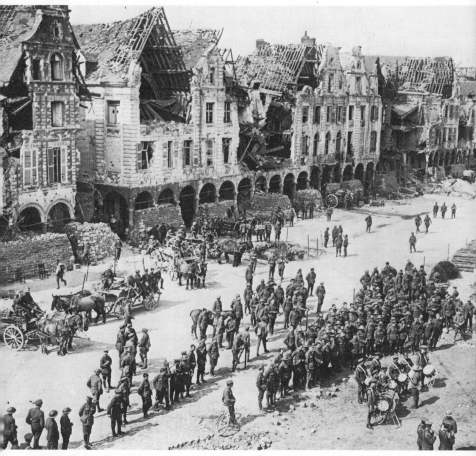

British military band playing in the Grande Place, Arras, 30 April 1917.
Imperial War Museum Q6407

After two or three nights of this waiting game we began to think
it was easy, but one night I was caught in a tree red-handed.
Jerry put up a flare and pasted the orchard. The hail of bullets
tore the branches and leaves like a scimitar. I was a sitting duck
all right, but none of the bullets was meant for me. The
sensation I endured up that tree is beyond my powers of
description. We were all bloody idiots, and dead lucky not to
suffer casualties.

The orchard screened a little villa which had had its roof
knocked off, though in happier days it was no doubt a charming
home for somebody. 'Whizz-Bang Villa' was chalked in giant

letters on one of the walls. Those of us not on gun duty crawled through the orchard to sleep on beds in the three bedrooms. The ground floor was covered with large black and white tiles, and provided quite a good game of shuffle board. It was a luxury to walk on a fine solid floor, instead of continually standing on dirt. A well-equipped kitchen gave us the chance to knock up a tasty feed, but we had to be careful about the smoke. The lads gave me full marks when I produced three big rissoles per man, made of bully and potatoes fried in swimming bacon fat. Real good they were. Stewed fruit was on the menu every day. This domesticity and housekeeping lark was rudely shattered every now and again when machine-gun bullets struck the walls, making us scuttle into the cellar like rabbits.

The brigade occupied that part of the line until 26 September. No attacks were made by either side and, except for a few bust-ups, things were reasonably quiet. I found a box of rifle-grenades, and Snowy and I decided to engage in a bit of pin-pricking with them. There were several ruined houses in Blairville close to the German front line; Jerries frequently hopped in and out of one particular building, which we suspected was being used as a cookhouse. Neither of us had been on a course about grenades but we had ideas, and set to work to try them out. The rifle-grenade resembled an elongated toffee-apple, with the case segmented for breaking up, shrapnel fashion. The rifle, loaded with a blank cartridge, was rested on the butt at a steep angle and the stick of the grenade placed in the muzzle. The removal of a pin freed a spinning vane which ensured that the grenade dropped nose-first. A calibrated quadrant was used to obtain the range. After a few experiments we proceeded to deliver the goods, and spent a pleasant hour knocking the ruins of Blairville about—and Jerries, too, we hoped.

Before we left Rivière some of us were pulled out of the line for a bombing course on the Mills bomb. I was fascinated by the neatness and power of that weapon, and when in the front line I usually carried one in each trouser pocket. It felt good to know that a bomb that could probably kill an elephant was immediately available on my person, in case of a surprise attack. I took good care to ensure that the striker of any Mills bomb I carried was well greased. It sometimes happened that no grease or mineral jelly was applied at the factory, with the result that the striker rusted up and the bomb would not function.

Great rumblings of gunfire began to be heard. On 28 September, after being relieved by the 41st Machine Gun Company, we boarded Paris buses. The brigade was on the move again. Taking a circuitous route via Doullens, we debussed near Albert and awaited orders. A new phase of the Somme battle had just developed, and on 1 October we marched through Longueval to Delville Wood, the scene of terrible fighting a few days earlier. The wood had been reduced to a vast mass of tree stumps and the shell-pocked ground was strewn with corpses. That night, Snowy's team and mine moved forward along a sunken road to strengthen the line at Gueudecourt. The road, which was banked on both sides, was full of British and German dead. In the darkness we kept stumbling over the bodies; when I fell heavily on one it gave out a deep grunt. The sudden weight of my body had compressed the corpse, forcing gases through the throat. I had heard of such a thing before but was a bit sceptical. Somebody laughed, but I felt far from laughter as I struggled to get the tripod on my shoulders once more. The sunken road ran straight to the front line, and Jerry light artillery plastered it continuously. The whole terrain for miles around had been a battle ground for weeks. Trônes Wood nearby, and the villages of Montauban, Guillemont and Flers had been flattened. Our big camouflaged guns were in the rolling valleys to the rear engaged in shelling Bapaume, a fair-sized town behind the German lines.

Stand-to was on when we slithered into the shallow front-line trench, there being no communicating approach trench. The Jerry shell-fire was so intense that an attack appeared imminent. The 6th Buffs were holding the line, and stretcher-bearers were giving first-aid to the wounded. I mounted the Vickers, loaded it and with some anxiety awaited developments. No Man's Land was no more than 120 yards across, and a sudden rush by the enemy would have brought them on top of us in less than half a minute. Presently an infantry officer hurried by and said that an attack on our line had started a little to the left. The enemy shelling suddenly stopped, an ominous warning. Without further ado I opened fire to discourage the development of any attack in front. In the darkness it was useless to wait until Jerry was on top of us. Snowy on my right quickly followed suit, and together we raked No Man's Land good and proper, snuffing out any attempt by the enemy to start an attack. Bombing was going on fifty yards to the left, but the Buffs held their ground and the attack failed. At frequent intervals during the night our two guns belted out, and gradually it seemed that we had gained the upper hand. Without the Vickers Jerry could have walked into our trench, as the infantry had suffered severe casualties.

Dawn came, and we were able to get our bearings. Behind the enemy front line rose a long low hill; the tallest building in Bapaume showed above the brow, sharply defined against the bright light from the east. A shout went up, and there, silhouetted in full view, were two German waggons drawn by pairs of horses. They were trying to make a get-away but had left it too late, a mistake Jerry frequently made.

I opened fire at a range of 400 yards, and the infantry joined in. Both waggons were quickly brought to a standstill. It was an unexpected bonus, but there was genuine regret about the animals.

Three days in that place exhausted us. What sleep we got had to be taken in odd snatches in an old German artillery dugout to the rear of the trench. I well remember Snowy fainting in that dugout, and it was some while before he recovered. Exhaustion had no doubt caused it, but at the time it shook me. I feared that he might lose some of the superb control he always showed, no matter how hard the conditions. He soon got over the slight set-back and became his old self once again. I think the incident worried me more than it did him. Two gun teams of 'A' Section relieved us on the fourth night, taking over our guns and ammo. As usual in such cases. I had an itemised receipt list ready for my opposite Number One to sign, showing that he had received the gun and stores.

The enemy shrapnel was hellish as we trudged back along the dreaded sunken road to the support lines near Delville Wood. When I was about to flop down with my companions to sleep, I discovered that I had lost my revolver. I remembered that I had felt something hit my foot a few yards before entering the sunken road and I informed an officer about the loss. He left it to me to decide whether I went back or not, at the same time mentioning seven pounds as the sum I might be called upon to

pay, failing recovery of the weapon. Bearing in mind that the
whole battle area was littered with war material worth millions
of quid, and that there was no apparent urgency to salvage it, the
officer's observation was a bit thick, to say the least. However,
with the possibility of a distasteful enquiry in the offing, plus my
boyish fears that ignominy would attach to such a loss, like a
mug I went back.

I soon found that being alone on the journey down the sunken
road was very different from being with my pals. Courage is
communicable from one to another. In company, the dangers
are shared, but when you are alone, amid darkness and the dead,
there is no sharing. The further I stumbled along the road the

Shrapnel bursting over Canadian troops in reserve trenches, 1916.
Imperial War Museum CO 806

more windy I became. There was some moonlight, but though it helped me to pick my way it more clearly showed the piles of corpses. My worst fear was being killed without a pal knowing about it. A pal would recover my paybook and, if he was sensible, pocket any cigarettes I had left as well as writing a letter of condolence to my next-of-kin, shown in the paybook as my mother. Perhaps he would find time to fix up a cross made of two bits of wood from an ammo box, and scrawl my name in indelible pencil on it the same as I had seen hundreds of names on similar crosses from time to time. I remembered a cross I had seen somewhere near Fosse 8, on which the inscription read 'Captain F Bowes-Lyon, Black Watch, 4th son of the Earl of Strathmore'.

Such fearsome thoughts were with me as I staggered towards the end of the sunken road, where the shrapnel bursts seemed to concentrate. One approaching shell burst twenty feet in front of me. As the hail of balls and fragments spattered the ground, I fell down, and for a moment I thought it was all over. Picking myself up, I ran like hell to get out of the road. Calculating the spot where I thought I had lost my revolver, I dropped on all fours and commenced crawling, feeling over the ground with both hands. Systematically I covered many square yards, up and down, up and down, convinced every minute that I was on a hopeless task and that I was a prize idiot. Then my hand touched a piece of cord; I knew instantly the revolver was attached to the other end of it. The cord was the lanyard, which in some inexplicable way had broken. What did it matter how it had happened, or how the weapon had tipped out of its holster, now that I had it firmly in my grasp?

On the way back I avoided the sunken road and struck across country. I strayed too far to the right and got lost, but some stretcher-bearers put me right and I found our support trench. Except for the sentries, the company was asleep. I had been away for four hours.

For three days we enjoyed comparative rest and quiet. Coal-boxes kept roaring overhead to Death Valley behind Delville Wood, searching for our heavy batteries, but we ignored them so long as they passed over at a good altitude. Near what remained of Flers was one of the first two tanks used in the war. Snowy and I put in a thorough inspection, marvelling at its apparent strength and formidable appearance. There it lay, knocked out by whizz-bangs, but its armament of four Vickers guns seemed to be in good condition. I will never understand what possessed our command to disclose that startling and revolutionary weapon to the Germans in such a puny thrust. It was not until fourteen months later that our tanks made an appearance in great strength. The premature disclosure at Flers politely told the German High Command that the Allies were thinking in terms of tanks as a means of breaking through.

A German Taube airplane came in low over our trench. The pilot leaned out and dropped a twenty-pound bomb, which failed to explode. Turning back to see what had happened, he was met by a long burst of fire from one of our guns, which had a tracer bullet in every fourth pocket of the belt. Tracer bullets were a new thing, and it was fascinating to watch their speed through the air. On this occasion the tracers seemed to be hitting the plane's engine, as the thin smoke they gave off was being whirled around by the propellers. The machine veered off in the direction of the front line, descending as it went. If the pilot made a safe landing in friendly territory he was a lucky man.

We went back to the front line again at Gueudecourt on 7 October. The sunken road was still under heavy shrapnel fire, and the officer in charge took us across country to avoid it. The front trench had been pounded for days and the Buffs had suffered many casualties. 'A' Section's four guns held the line for two days to ease the strain on the Buffs. The whizz-bangs were unbearable, and several of our gunners became casualties. Jock Tait, a big Scot in my team, was struck plumb in the centre of the forehead by a shrapnel ball. The hole was bigger than a sixpence, and perfectly round. Owing to the events which followed, I'm afraid that I don't know whether he survived. I would be most happy to learn that he did.

We were relieved after dark on 10 October and, loaded like pack mules, slogged it back to Death Valley, where huts constructed of sandbags with tin roofs had been erected for the troops to rest in. We had a good deal of freedom, and Snowy and I meandered about enjoying life, thankful that we had so far been spared. We sometimes felt a little small when we watched the big guns do their stuff and compared them with the Vickers. Yet we knew that under certain conditions the Vickers was the more deadly. The story of David and Goliath had a special appeal for us. In those far-off days, although we were still only kids, dealing out death was our business. Our homeland desired it and had trained us for that very purpose. Whatever the rights or wrongs of the war, and we didn't know much about all that, we were in it up to our necks for better or worse.

23 My number was on it

And now I come to a totally unexpected turning-point in my story, one of those things you could bank on never happening but which do. It was nearly 2 pm on 17 October and we were about to parade for revolver inspection before returning to the line at Gueudecourt. A whistle blew, and as 'A' Section moved out of the hut for parade I was shot through the left foot by a .45 bullet from Snowy's revolver. The bullet tore between two bones in front on the ankle, went out through the instep of my boot and buried itself in the ground. With his revolver pointing downwards, and not realising that it was loaded, Snowy had casually pulled the trigger and Wham! I was out of the fighting for six months. There was pandemonium for a few moments as I hobbled about in pain, and then I found myself on the back of a comrade named Grigg, who carried me to a field dressing station close by. Poor Snowy was put under open arrest pending an enquiry. I'll never forget how at first I was in an acute state of alarm at the unorthodox manner in which I had become a casualty. After many months of shot and shell from the enemy, with every missile carrying possible death or mutilation, it was shattering to find myself hors de combat through the unwitting agency of my best pal.

That evening, with other wounded men, I travelled in a very ancient char-à-banc past the ruins of Montauban and Longueval, right out of the battle area. The further I went, the more my spirits rose, as it gradually dawned on me that I was surely the luckiest Tommy in the whole of France. My hopes soared at the prospect of getting to Blighty, and I felt immense relief as I moved from the danger zone.

I was puzzled, on being transferred to an ambulance car, to find myself the only casualty in it. Finally I arrived at the 39th

Casualty Clearing Station. Next morning I discovered that there was something queer about the place, which filled me with misgivings. None of the nursing staff appeared friendly, and the matron looked, and was, a positive battle-axe. I made anxious enquiries, and quickly learned that I was classed as a suspected self-inflicted-wound case. Unknown to me, the letters SIW with a query mark added had been written on the label attached to my chest. Here was a fine kettle of fish, and I was in a state of near-panic. The place was full of SIW cases, or suspected cases, and normal standards of kindness were not allowed to nurture there. Many cases of wounding, even blindness, had been caused by foolish curiosity or needless tampering with detonators, fuses, rusted-up bombs and other weapons away from the trenches. That alone cast dark suspicion on the unlucky victim, who, by carelessness, as opposed to a genuine accident, fell into the fearful SIW category. Whenever it was possible for a patient to do any kind of chore, he was set to work. If he had lost a foot, he could brood over his misfortune while peeling spuds, or any other task that he was able to do without the aid of two feet.

One man told me that he had been tampering with what he thought was a dud bomb, and had lost his right hand. Of course, there were patients who had deliberately injured themselves in order to avoid further fighting. These were the blackest among those black sheep. The poor devils must have been in a dreadful state of mind to savage themselves, but I doubt whether severe mental stress was taken into account when pleading for mercy at the court martial which awaited them all.

In every unit there were always one or two men who were below standard, unable to control or hide their fears in times of danger. To be blunt, they ought not to have been soldiers at all, yet they volunteered for service. Events, however, proved too much for them, and they were to be pitied.

Three most anxious days passed. A report about me was received at last, and I was given clearance, thus ending the most unpleasant of my war experiences. All smiles again, and with my foot not troubling me unduly, I travelled to Rouen, where I was earmarked for Blighty. On 23 October I was aboard the hospital ship *Western Australia*. The wooded banks of the Seine were in a blaze of autumn colour as we set out on the eight-hour journey down to Le Havre. Everything was so peaceful and quiet that it seemed to belong to another world. It was a happy trip, with sing-songs and good eating.

> Today's my daughter's wedding day. Hooray!
> Fifty thousand pounds I'll give away. Hooray!

I was amazed to be given two bottles of Guinness to drink. At Southampton, a crowd of uniformed angels hovered around with lashings of sandwiches, drinks and cigarettes. It is not easy to find the right words to describe my feelings then. I leave it to the reader to imagine.

24 Blighty

There was a delay at Southampton while the wounded were sorted out for various hospitals. The aim seemed to be to send patients as far from their homes as possible. My home was in Croydon, but I was packed off to Bridgenorth Hospital, Shropshire. Scotsmen were almost certain to drop anchor in the south, and so on. Maybe it was to discourage or reduce travel by relatives, as railways were the only means of long-distance transport then. Would it not have been better and wiser to send men to hospitals as near as possible to their homes, to save relatives a lot of expense and the railways an unnecessary burden?

However, I have nothing but the happiest of memories of Bridgenorth Hospital. I secretly fell in love with most of the nurses—they looked so beautiful—but I was a bit too shy then, my social contact with girls before the war having been almost nil. It was a wonderful thing being a wounded Tommy, and I lapped up the attentions of the visitors like a young puppy. The personal feeling of health and cleanliness, and the good food, were sheer luxury to men who had almost forgotten what civilisation was like.

And so to Hereford, to finish my convalescence at a private hospital, where a Lady Butler reigned like a queen of matrons. She was tall, dark and handsome, and invariably dressed in a scarlet silk habit, obviously of her own personal choice. She looked like a female cardinal, and the rustle of her dress gave considerable warning of her approach. She was no battle-axe, but a very gracious person, and she more than fulfilled the preconceived notions I had as to what a titled lady should look like and how she should behave. I was dead lucky to have struck that hospital. I'll never forget the food and perquisites we Tommies had there. Her Ladyship personally issued the daily ration of twenty cigarettes or an ounce of pipe tobacco per man. On my nineteenth birthday, I had a surprise birthday cake.

The best Hereford people vied with each other to entertain us. I remember one wonderful tea at the home of the Bulmers, the famous cider family. On another occasion some of us took tea in a big country mansion where there was a bowling green; our instructor in the game was Admiral Sir Reginald Tyrwhitt-Wilson, a famous sailor of the time. Once I had cast away my crutches, rides in grand old motor cars were mine for the asking. Theatres, whist drives, concerts, bun-fights—we had the lot.

The fractures in my foot mended, the bullet hole disappeared, and within four months I was able to walk about as if nothing had happened. Lady Butler kept her boys as long as she could, but an RAMC doctor made frequent visits, and at last she had to sign me off. It was a sad day for me when I left Hereford.

25 A1 again

The party was now over, and after some sick leave I reported to Harrowby Camp, Grantham, on the estate of Lord Brownlow. The camp was the principal training base of the Machine Gun Corps. In a matter of hours, the memory of the soft time in hospital was purged from me into a half-forgotten dream. Stiff training was started at once, with spit and polish, guard duties, fatigues and whatnot thrown in. After the cushy time in hospital we soon had good cause to moan and groan. Our particular bane was a bunch of fire-eating instructors from the Guards, none of whom had actual fighting knowledge—they were mere parade-ground tyrants. We ex-wounded types were quickly told to forget any experience acquired in France, as it counted for nothing at Harrowby.

One of the instructors warned us, 'Any bloody lip from any of yer and I'll whip him straight off to the guard room.' 'Oh, what a bastard,' I muttered under my breath, and the bloke next to me croaked, 'By Christ, if ever I meet that bastard in France, I'll blow his bloody guts out.' Our ranks seethed with rage. Even I, young as I was, regarded myself as an old soldier, a fighting soldier, and entitled to some slight recognition of the fact. Such calculated and insufferable insolence—it was nothing less—was hard to bear, and it was not only our particular bully who was chucking his weight about; they were all at it. I must have been growing fast, I was that bloody mad.

There was no escape. Fitness was literally lashed into us, but our indignation remained. Every week names were called for overseas drafts, meaning goodbye to pints in Grantham on Friday nights, fish and chips, and feeds in church institutes with nice girls to serve us. I was on a draft sooner than I expected, and within a few days arrived at Folkestone, mighty glad to get away from that bunch of blow-hards at Harrowby. It was 9 April 1917, and I didn't know that the battle of Arras had just commenced, with ice and snow on the ground. Rough weather prevented us from sailing, but on 17 April I arrived at Camiers, a reception base for drafts.

The days passed with training at full blast, including passing through the gas hut a few times. Very soon, records showed that seven men were earmarked for a draft to the 12th Division; I was among them. On the day for entraining, the RSM called out the names of the senior NCO destined for each particular division, who then stepped forward and took charge of his draft. When he came to the 12th Division draft list, the RSM yelled out, 'Private Coppard, step forward ten paces, turn and face your men.' In a daze, I did as I was told, and then learned that as there were no NCOs for the 12th Division the senior private would take charge. And so it fell to me to draw a blanket and three days' rations for myself and six men. None of the six had been overseas before. When I became used to the idea, I felt a bit cocky. I was psychologically superior to the six, but without a stripe to back it up.

The rations were placed in a box, and I knew they would have to be watched. One of my draft was a trouble-maker, a good ten years older than I was, a hungry-gutted type. When we boarded the train he demanded his whack of rations, although the others were content to let them stay in the box. He made it plain that he trusted nobody. At first I refused his demand, but the blighter kept up his pestiferous and anti-social nagging. In the end I succumbed, and doled out the rations equally between the lot of us. The journey was long-winded, broken by stops at various camps. On the third day, the trouble-maker was rationless and begging for a crust. 'You've bloody well had it, mate,' I said, but good-natured mugs that we were, we each gave him a bit of this and that to see him through.

Leaving the train at Frévent, we marched to the 6th Corps reinforcement camp and joined the 12th Division reserve battalion, thus ending my brief taste of petty authority. I was very pleased to learn that I was to return to the 37th Machine Gun Company. For several days all available troops were employed in digging trenches round the camp, ostensibly for defence in case of a German break-through, though more likely this was a subterfuge to keep our minds and muscles occupied. Suddenly the 12th Division draft moved off and arrived in the stricken city of Arras. The sixteenth-century town hall in Barbed Wire Square was a heap of stones.

26 I rejoin the 37th Machine Gun Company

I was the sole reinforcement for my old company, and a guide took me to rear HQ. Jerry shells were crumping down in parts of the city when I reported my arrival. It was 8 May 1917, and the British attack to clear the enemy from the environs of Arras had ground to a halt a few kilometres east along the Cambrai road. During my absence in Blighty there had been a change in the company command. Captain Anderson was divisional CO in charge of machine gun companies, with the rank of major. The strange faces at HQ made me a little upset, but before I had time to turn round I was on my way to the reserve trenches at Feuchy, where I joined some of my old companions in 'A' Section. I was happy to be with them again, and they plied me with countless questions about the old homeland. They were naturally envious of my good fortune in having had six months' freedom from danger and misery, but there was no mistaking the warmth of their welcome. They had suffered a hard winter and were battle-weary.

Two of my old pals had been killed, Armstrong and Marshall. The latter had vanished from the scene and nobody knew what had happened to him. It was presumed he had been buried by a shell, a fate suffered by many Tommies. Soon I met Snowy Hankin, now promoted to full corporal; he never mentioned the accident in which we had both been so closely involved. I gathered he was a bit touchy about the subject, and I was glad enough to let sleeping dogs lie. Very few of 'A' Section had been on leave to Blighty. They all had an intense longing for leave, and I know some feared that death might cheat them. I also learned with much regret that Lieutenant Clarke, the first commander of my old platoon in the Queen's, had been killed.

My diary for 9 May reads, 'Very fine day and plenty of air fights.' The air power of both the Germans and the Allies had increased considerably, and anti-aircraft gunnery was a permanent feature of the war scene. I was soon posted to a gun team, but before joining it I went up the line to supplement a neighbouring gun team on the right bank of the Scarpe canal. The two gun positions were located close together beside the water. As things were quiet at that particular time the officer permitted several of us to go for a swim. We set off towards a bend in the canal about a hundred yards from the gun positions. When we were well round the bend I saw some other swimmers in the water about two hundred yards away. Suddenly one of my companions yelled, 'Blimey! They're bloody Jerries!' And so they were. We turned tail at speed, making a bit of a splash. They must have had a man on guard, for I heard the crack of a rifle and a bullet struck the canal bank above our heads.

The battle of Arras was still going on, and a show was working up to capture ground near Roeux. On 12 May our artillery put up a fierce bombardment and our two guns joined in with barrage fire across the canal on Jerry's support area. The 37th Brigade attacked, and later a big party of Jerries, carrying no visible arms, swarmed down the other side of the canal. Suddenly they saw us, and up shot their hands. Our guns were trained on them, and it was touch and go whether to open fire, but they were too far from their own lines to get back if they had any trickery in mind similar to that perpetrated on 'B' Company of the Queen's in the Hohenzollern Redoubt. One or two of us favoured the extreme treatment, but Lieutenant W D Garbutt decided they should be taken prisoner. A big punt lay nearby, and the officer ordered the Jerries to cross over to our side but they stood with their hands up and wouldn't budge. No doubt with our two machine guns and cocked revolvers we looked a menacing lot. In the end a party of the Queen's rounded them up. Lieutenant Garbutt, a Yorkshireman I believe, was in charge of 'A' Section then. He was courageous, steady and companionable, and we thought a lot of him.

The 12th Division, which had been in the line since the start of the battle on 9 April, had a hard-earned rest due to it, so I was fortunate in rejoining my old unit at that time. Although I had been with the section only a few days I soon fell into the old routine. My sudden plunge into the fighting area again brought back that wind-up feeling under shell-fire, and it was not easy to control. The daily comradeship of my pals, whether in or out of the line, gave me strength. To most of us it was not a matter of patriotism any longer—that had burned itself out long ago. What remained was a silent bonding together of men who knew there was no other way out but to see the thing through. Deep down, too, was an implacable hatred of the Huns, for all the misery and death they had caused. It would have been un-British not to want to settle the score with them.

We cleaned up in Arras, and then marched via Duisans to Montenescourt, where General Scott presented medal ribbons. I studied these closely. The French *Croix de Guerre* was much in evidence, and I saw one or two men with the Russian Order of St George. I was nineteen years old then, and to win a medal of some sort was my highest ambition. There were medal-scoffers of course, who jeered about medals being sent up with the rations, but I'm sure that every man in his heart would have liked a medal, if only to relieve the monotony of the uniform.

The brigade was transported in motor lorries to Avesne-le-Comte and dispersed to neighbouring villages for billeting. Our company rested in the little village of Oppy and got down to cleaning and training right away. I was a Number One again. After a week of intensive gun drill a competition was held. The officers put up some money, and my team won ten francs for speed in mounting the gun and knocking down a steel plate at 200 yards' range. Our time of 27 seconds gives some idea of the kind of drill Major Anderson was keen on. We blew the ten francs that night on wine. At half a franc a bottle we were soon reduced to a maudlin condition.

Two of my team had joined the company while I was in Blighty. One was Edwin Short and the other was Jock Hershell. Edwin was born in the Argentine and came from there to enlist. His father was English and his mother Spanish. He had had a university education and spoke perfect English, and I never understood why he wasn't an officer. Like his name, he was short and tubby, and also looked a bit untidy, which often got him into hot water. But any man who travels over 6,000 miles to fight for his father's homeland is no ordinary man. Jock, of course, was a Scot, very broad and strong, and a splendid companion.

27 12th Division sports

On 1 June, the second anniversary of our arrival in France, the company went on a long route march in light order, with sing-songs all the way. Next day company sports were held. Although I was no athlete, I entered the sack race for a lark. To my astonishment I won first prize, a ten-franc voucher, exchangeable at the divisional canteen. Ivergny was the venue for the brigade sports and, fancying myself as a sack pedestrian, I decided to compete. The result was that I dead-heated with a chap in the Queen's, the first and second prizes being shared between us. Divisional sports soon followed at Grand Rullecourt and I just had to enter the sack race. In fact I was practically ordered to compete and was given permission to train with the real athletes, being excused all parades to do so. Fired by my previous successes, insignificant and comic though they were, I suppose it was the first time in my young life that I really set out to win something. My enthusiasm and the improvement in my performance caught the eye of officers and NCOs alike, and I was encouraged on all sides. Gradually I realised that these gentry also had an eye to business, for they saw a chance of winning a packet of money.

Sports day arrived, and off we competitors went, packed in a limber drawn by a couple of mules. The sports were held in the grounds of a château, where the 36th Machine Gun Company kindly provided dinner. The sun shone, and a big crowd of Frenchies were present, as well as troops. There were also a number of bookies, dressed up like the real thing, complete with cigars, grey bowlers and money bags. How they got their impedimenta into France was a mystery. Obviously they were bookies in civvy street. They shouted the odds for the various events in real professional style, and ten to one was offered for all competitors in the sack race. A good deal of cash was placed on me and the bookies smelt a rat. Down came the price, but all the same they were well caned when I romped home by a clear twenty yards.

I couldn't go wrong that day. Officers and NCOs patted me on the back as they handed me more beer than I could drink.

In a thicket away from the general view were a number of casks of beer, around which was a swarm of NCOs. Sir Julian Byng, the new commander of the Third Army, was present. Silver medals in the shape of the ace of spades were given to first-prize winners in all events, plus a ten-franc voucher. So ended a happy day, long to be remembered.

28 The Arras struggle

On 18 June the company marched in full kit to Gouy-en-Artois. The next day we proceeded to Arras, where we operated from Shamrock Corner. We were in reserve, and from time to time odd jobs of carrying and maintenance fell to us. On several occasions I helped to repair the front-line wire, a nerve-racking job. Dreading bursts of machine-gun fire, we worked in silence at top pressure until dawn crept up. We made many trips carrying boxes of small arms ammo up to the front line, a journey of over two miles. Each box contained 1,000 rounds of ammo. The last quarter of a mile under severe shell-fire was cruel, and I was drenched in sweat.

Occasionally we were allowed to visit Arras, where the open-air swimming bath was a great attraction. The 'Spades' concert party ran a show in the city. A pretty soprano sang 'Little Brown Bird' and 'Roses in Picardy'. So sentimental was her rendering that she nearly had me in tears.

Reserve duties ended, and 'A' Section took over a part of the

Wancourt Line, on the right of the Arras-Cambrai road. Not far from us, on the left of the road at the top of a low hill, were the remains of Monchy-le-Preux, where the cavalry had been cut up in the early stages of the battle. My pals told me that the cavalry attack had been a fiasco. It is impossible to understand the reason for throwing horse cavalry against machine guns skilfully emplaced behind a screen of barbed wire. If it was in the nature of an experiment or test to see what would happen, then whoever gave the order received a salutary lesson. The attack was a suicidal failure.

German shelling in the Wancourt area was the heaviest I had yet experienced. In addition to employing many howitzer batteries firing coal-boxes, Jerry was using a 17-inch howitzer which fired a shell weighing over a ton. The missile approached

British troops marching through Arras, 14 April 1917.
Imperial War Museum Q3094

with a roar like an express train and petrified us as it shot over our heads, before plunging on the outskirts of Monchy with a shattering explosion.

I had a nasty shaking-up on 3 July. Coal-boxes were coming over in fours; on that fine summer evening we counted 180, all of them dropping within a 200-yard radius of our position. There was no difficulty in picking them out in the clear evening sky just before the final drop, and it was hair-raising to try to forecast a positive threat to our little section of trench. Miraculously my team suffered no casualties, but the next evening poor Edwin was killed outright. When the shelling lulled a bit, three of us took him to a patch near Fosse Farm, and, I'm afraid, buried him in great haste, for the blasted Hun began dropping crumps almost on the place. 'Goodbye, old pal,' were the only words said. We planted crossed sticks in the mud and then hurried back to the front trench.[1]

I remember that another of my chaps, named Ellis, was struck between his shoulder blades by a piece of shrapnel. We ripped open the back of his tunic and there was the lump of iron exposed to view, half embedded in the flesh just clear of the vertebrae. When I attempted to pull it out with my fingers I found it was too hot to hold.

On 7 July my team crossed the Cambrai road to take over a gun position close to Monchy. We were soon engaged in anti-aircraft duty. As the size of the German air force grew, so their pilots were getting bolder. It became common practice for them

---

[1] In 1977, I received a letter from Mr Thomas H. Webster of Southsea, Hampshire. 'I was amazed,' he wrote, 'to see my cousin's name mentioned in your book . . . I was fourteen when he was killed so I remember him very well: he used to spend his leave with us in Bristol. You are quite correct in all the details you mentioned . . . he must have told you all about himself. His father was my mother's brother and his mother was a beautiful Spanish lady. Edwin was the only boy in a family of five girls. He was strongly advised not to go to England to join the army, especially as he was an Argentine by birth, but he was determined to fight for his father's country. When he first joined up he was in the Queen's Royal West Surrey Regiment and he was very proud of his cap badge—a lamb! I well remember that when we saw him off on the train at Bristol station in 1917 he was very depressed and was certain he would not be back again. It was during this leave, his last, that we had the sad job of telling him that his mother had died recently, which upset him very much . . . I have a vivid recollection of the day we received notification of his death in a letter from an officer, Lieutenant Hudson, I believe. It was a great shock to us but especially to his father in Buenos Aires. He came to visit us in 1927 and then went to France to see Edwin's grave at Windmill British Cemetery, Monchy.'

to strafe our infantry with machine guns, a menace that had to be countered. Like the latest Allied aircraft of that time, some German machines were fitted with a mechanism that enabled the pilot to fire machine guns through the propellers with great accuracy.

For anti-aircraft work a circular pit was dug and the Vickers mounted on a post in the centre. This allowed a full circle of fire. Enemy airmen were quick to notice that there was a blind spot directly above the gun, which would not operate at too steep an angle. A sharp lookout had to be kept. Provided one put in a good burst as an enemy aircraft approached, it would veer off at once or take refuge in the clouds. Once, a Boche plane sneaked up from behind, and from 200 feet up dropped a twenty-pound bomb, which only missed us by a few feet. As the pilot sped off on a straight course, not a brilliant thing to do, I helped him on his way with a long burst, which included tracers. He crossed No Man's Land only a few feet up, and the infantry peppered him for all they were worth.

There was a rumour in the company that if a gunner brought down an enemy plane a reward of 500 francs and ten days' leave would be given. We heard nothing official about it and I think it was just boloney. How could a gunner prove a claim, when most of the infantry were having a bash too? After all, a single bullet in the right place might do the trick.

I got in a spot of bother one day when a fight between one of our planes and a Jerry was going on. The Iron Cross marking was quite distinct on the enemy machine as it weaved in and out of the low clouds; equally clear was the circular tricolour on the RFC plane. Both planes were shooting at each other and playing hide-and-seek, and I took a hand in the game by belting at Jerry whenever I spotted him. Suddenly our company CO appeared at my side and yelled, 'What the bloody hell do you think you are doing? You're shooting at a British machine. Consider yourself under open arrest.' But a few moments later we heard the noise of one of the planes, and there was Jerry, with the Iron Cross badge as black as the ace of spades. The CO stood beside me as I promptly gave the enemy plane a good burst before it could reach cloud cover again; and that was the last we saw of it. Very sportingly the CO said, 'That was a Jerry all right. Sorry,' and off he went.

At 5 am on 11 July the enemy made a strong attack on Long Trench on our left, capturing 150 yards of it. For three hours there was hand-to-hand fighting and bombing, but by 8 am the enemy had been driven out, leaving many dead behind as well as prisoners. During the raid, in response to an SOS signal from our front line, I fired 1,500 rounds on the enemy's front line and support trenches, thus adding to the general hate that fine evening.

It was on this occasion that we ran out of water for the Vickers. Our reserve supply had disappeared and there was very little drinking water left in our water bottles. As a temporary measure all the members of my team piddled into the water jacket of the gun through a funnel, to the accompaniment of much hilarity and many vulgar remarks. As it was midsummer the natural sources of supply were very meagre, but with the help of other troops sufficient water was obtained to get the gun going again. The only drawback was the offensive odour.

In the afternoon a fierce dog-fight took place overhead, when four Boche planes singled out one of ours and shot it down. It landed in No Man's Land in front of our gun position. To our surprise, the airman climbed out and started to hobble towards us. To cover him, I plastered the enemy parapet in a broad sweeping traverse, and the airman managed to roll into a shell hole near a gap in our wire. Very soon a whizz-bang battery set about destroying the crippled plane, putting about fifty shells around it. Finally it burnt itself out. The wounded pilot wisely stayed in the shell hole and was brought in at dusk.

I developed a nasty boil on the nape of my neck and went to the first-aid post to get it lanced. There was no sticking plaster available and, owing to the awkward position of the boil, I was bandaged around the neck, jaws and forehead. It looked as if my head had been blown off. My afflicted appearance drew attention as I trudged back to the front line. One Tommy, no doubt thinking I was off my rocker as well as badly wounded, laid a restraining hand on my shoulder and said, 'Hey, mate, aren't you going the wrong way?' I had a high temperature and my head was rocking as I made my way back to the front line.

Suddenly I ran into a party of staff officers accompanying Sir Julian Byng, GOC the Third Army, on a tour of inspection. I wondered if I was seeing things. When about to pass by me, the general, noticing my bandaged head, stopped and said, 'Are you wounded?' I replied, 'No sir.' 'Boils?' queried the general. 'Yes sir,' I said, hoping that he, in an expansive mood, would wave a hand and say, 'Send this boy down to reserve for a couple of days' rest.' I had no such luck. 'Beastly things. I've had them myself,' he said, and with that the general and his entourage moved on.

News passed round that Major Anderson had been killed. I was sad and surprised, as I had pictured him directing the operations of his machine gunners from a safe distance. I was wrong. If I had seriously considered the matter, I would have realised that Major Anderson not only gave orders, but was the type of officer who, when occasion demanded it, would want to see them carried out.

I feel I must mention a piece of psychological propaganda, put about by some War Office person, which brought poor comfort to Tommies. The story swept the world and, being gullible, we in the trenches were taken in by it for a while. With slight variations it indicated that the German war industry was in a bad way, and was short of fats for making glycerine. To overcome the shortage a vast secret factory had been erected in the Black Forest, to which the bodies of dead British soldiers were dispatched. The bodies, wired together in bundles, were pitchforked on to conveyor belts and moved into the factory for conversion into fats. War artists and cartoonists got busy, and dreadful scenes were depicted and published in Britain.

The effect on me at first was one of morbid despondency. Death was not enough apparently. The idea of finishing up in a stew pot was bloody awful, but as I had so many immediate problems the story soon lost its evil potency for me. We called the Germans a lot of bloody bastards, but I think it safe to say that if the object of the story was to work the British troops into a state of fighting frenzy, then it was a complete and utter wash-out. Tommy was giving all he could, and no more was left, except his life. The reader who has not heard of this story before should know that the individual at the War Office responsible for this dirty bit of propaganda admitted some twenty years or more later that the whole thing was a pack of lies from start to finish.

'A' Section was relieved on 13 July and went back to

Shamrock Corner. I well remember an old German notice-board at the side of the road. It read: *Zum Tilloy—Kronprinz Rupprecht Weg*. The notice intrigued us and we had fun in saying the words as gutturally as we could. 'Who is this bloke Rupprecht?' someone asked, but none of us really knew. It is of interest to note that this Crown Prince, eldest son of Louis III, King of Bavaria, was in command at that very time of several German armies, one of which was doing its best to wipe out the 12th Division at Monchy.

In our reserve capacity we became maids of all work again, humping, wiring, digging and so on, but I was suddenly whipped off to become guide and temporary batman to a newly-joined Second Lieutenant X. I had a new stripe, for I was an unfledged and unpaid lance-corporal. I took the young officer to a reserve trench close to the front line at Monchy. Enemy shelling provided a sticky reception, and we found shelter in the

German signpost in Tilloy, April 1917, remembered by the author.
Imperial War Museum Q1999

entrance of a collapsed dugout. Mr X was two or three years older than I was, but I felt responsible for teaching him the ways of trench life. In a matter of hours I realised, to my alarm, that he was mentally and physically incapable of making good. It was tough luck that his first taste of trench warfare was under such heavy shell-fire. I searched around and found a deeper dugout, but once he was in I couldn't get him out of it. Arguing, pleading, cajoling, almost threatening, made no difference; he wouldn't budge. The poor devil was paralysed with fear. Wounded men and stretcher-bearers took shelter on the steps of the dugout, which made matters worse for him. Not even the urge of nature would tempt him out of the place, and he did his business there. He lost his appetite and wouldn't touch the tasty bits I fixed up for him. Once, when I went to fetch rations from the rear, I returned to find the dugout full of badly-wounded men, but the young officer had done nothing to help them. He kept me well supplied with cigarettes but I was obliged to empty his slops. At times, to my embarassment, he would burst into tears. I felt that the situation was quite beyond me but I had to stick it for more than a week and was jolly glad when it was over. It wasn't long before the CO and his brother officers realised that they had a dud officer reinforcement, and within a month he reported sick with a blister on his heel. He never came back to the company. I've often wondered what strings were pulled to get rid of him.

At one time there was a chap in my gun team who suffered in much the same way, but he had to stick it and he led a hell of a life. As he had an ungainly hump on his back and a cast in his eye, his appearance was rather repellent, and he had an appetite like a wolf. He was cursed with a physique that drew scorn upon him. Once, someone referring to the hump called out, 'Why don't you put that little bleeder down and give him a walk?' That poor blighter had trouble all right, and all because nature had not endowed him with sufficient strength of character and will to overcome his physical defects.

On 2 August a heavy concentration of shells rained down on a support trench north of Monchy where 'A' Section's guns were mounted. This was followed by mortar fire on the infantry in the front line. At 9.30 pm Jerry infantry attacked in mass, and our hard-pressed defenders sent up SOS signals. The section's four guns answered the call at once with barrage fire on the enemy support areas. My target was a wood called Bois du Sart, where it was known enemy troops were concentrated. We maintained our fire for three hours, drawing on to ourselves a deluge of gas shells. Our new box-type respirators were efficient, but after an hour's use the discomfort was overpowering. As soon as the all-clear signal shot up into the night sky I tore off my mask. Word soon came that Jerry had been repulsed with heavy losses.

From 6 to 12 August the company rested in tents at Beurains and we were able to visit Arras in the evenings. Carousing was the best medicine for battle-weary soldiers. The wine acted quickly, but overshadowing our rest was the haunting thought of the next spell up the line. Every return to the trenches was a new battle for the individual Tommy. It mattered little to him what was going on at other parts of the front. His fight was chiefly against the fears within himself and a few days' rest was not enough to restore his morale. Just as he was beginning to feel some benefit, he was back in the front line again. The thunder of guns in the distance made him say, 'I pity those poor bleeders up there,' but he still had his own worries to contend with. The magnitude of a great battle stirred his blood, but there were many long and lonely hours of sentry vigil at night, when, in his imaginings, phantasmagorical Jerries swarmed across No Man's Land in fearsome numbers.

My gun team and another took over a two-gun emplacement, with dugout, in Spade Trench on 13 August. The main entrance led down to a chamber. Two shafts gave access to the guns, which were twenty feet apart at ground level. Although the chamber was no more than twelve feet deep, it had three possible exits. Heavy thunderstorms occurred, putting a damper on things generally for a few days, and there was a distinct lull in the fighting. But on 17 August heavy shelling started again in our vicinity.

Jock Hershell left the dugout during the shelling and didn't return for a while. I became apprehensive and went along to a latrine sap where I thought he might be. I found him there, slumped in a heap, severely wounded. We carried him into the dugout. At a glance I saw that his broad back had caught a blast of shrapnel. I slit his tunic and underclothes with a jack-knife and separated them. I winced at the sight. Jock's back was full of punctures, and blood bubbles were wheezing out of the holes as he breathed. Our hearts sank and we feared the worst. The backs of his powerful upper arms hung in shreds. He appeared to be in no pain, though he was anxious and kept asking the extent of the injuries he could not see. We lied like hell and gave him first-aid, using nearly all our bandages and iodine in the process. 'You've got a Blighty one for sure,' I cried.

It seemed hours before we got him away to a first-aid post, where we left him, knowing that we would never see him again. Strong as he was, he could not survive his terrible injuries, and he died shortly afterwards. Farewell once more to a brave and staunch comrade. In a small unit like a machine gun team, it was a deep and personal loss when a comrade was killed and the bond of friendship broken for ever.

At that stage of the war in 1917 the build-up of German artillery was immense, and in the Monchy area the shell-fire seldom stopped. When Jerry searched and found the range of a trench he saturated it. Why we survivors weren't driven dotty, I'll never know. Never once did I hear the order, 'Retire,' and no one expected to hear it. There were many occasions when I think it would have been wiser to evacuate a position in order to prevent unnecessary slaughter, but the unwritten code was, 'There you are, and there you stay,' or as Tommy put it, 'We're here, because we're here.'

I have often thought that the words of Tennyson, 'Theirs not to reason why, theirs but to do and die', have been indirectly responsible for many a British soldier's death. The words were a godsend to generals and fireside lancers, but they brought small comfort to those who had to do the fighting. The epic charge which inspired Tennyson probably only lasted a few minutes. To apply the same code in the trenches month after month was demanding a hell of a lot, but the Tommies did accept the spirit of Tennyson's words, to their everlasting credit.

By now the reader has most likely heard enough about the final stages of the Third Battle of Arras as I saw it. From September to early November the company continued in and out of the Monchy and Wancourt lines, with no promise of a breakthrough. Fierce artillery and mortar duels blasted the earth with cruel monotony, and the 37th Brigade was hard hit. Jerry got it in the neck even worse from our Stokes mortar gun, which had an amazing speed of delivery. A barrage from a battery of Stokes mortars was a deadly business. With twenty or more bombs in the air at any one time, they literally rained down on the enemy target.

Big British raids were developing too, the purpose being to kill, create panic and snatch prisoners. Many special volunteers, tough and resolute, were used in a single raid. They were exempted from ordinary duties and had good rests between operations. Officered by young and intrepid types, they were trained to perfection in bombing and bayonet work. Their plans were secret, and only when they swarmed into a sector of the line did the local troops know that there was trouble afoot. At first glance you couldn't tell the difference between officers and other ranks. All wore privates' uniforms, badges of rank being neatly sewn on just below the back of the tunic collar. Their faces blackened, they tossed back tots of rum. Then, like gladiators, they were ready to strike. Cutters prepared the way where the wire was thinnest, and the raiders streaked across No Man's Land like ghosts in the darkness to pounce on the unsuspecting Jerries. In ten minutes or so it would all be over, and they returned with a batch of frightened prisoners, leaving the local troops the burden of enemy retaliation.

I see that I was promoted corporal in October, in place of Corporal Bernard, who had been sent on a course at the base and had not returned. This made me the senior corporal of the company, with a tidy bit of back pay in the offing. My pay then reached eleven shillings a week.

29 The Battle of Cambrai

The beginning of November found the division engaged on intense training and manoeuvres in open country around Frévent. The weather was cold and wet, and I contracted influenza, which put me in hospital for eight days. The rest between clean sheets was out of this world, and for a while I was lice-free. When I returned to my unit I received a slight shock by being made orderly sergeant for a week. I soon learned that something big was working up: in fact, the tank assault on Cambrai.

At midnight on 19 November the company left the village of Heudicourt and moved towards the front line near Gonnelieu. The division had become fighting fit again. Large drafts had made up some of the losses from the Arras struggle. Our company was at full strength with 16 guns, but nearly half the complement were newcomers. The CO for the task before us was Major B R Delbos, who was, I believe, a Frenchman by birth. I never got to know him very well, but he sent me a kindly letter later on, which I still have.

It was common knowledge that the division was about to take part in the most sensational attack in military history. The Third Army was to strike the enemy in the wake of a battering ram of over 400 tanks. I was a corporal in charge of two guns, each with a lance-corporal as Number One. The assembly point for the 37th Brigade, commanded by Brigadier-General Cator, was approximately 600 yards south-west of Gonnelieu. Nearly 4,000 men were quietly brought together, each of the four battalions being guided to its appointed place. The night was pitch black, and smoking was absolutely prohibited. Officers had instructions to shoot any man caught smoking. There we were, a brigade of men, shivering on a cold November night, without a smoke, and suffering like drug addicts. Talking had to be restrained to the utmost, and then we were only allowed to communicate in whispers. It was the queerest sensation being packed with a vast crowd of warriors, within 400 yards of our front line, and out in the open, after living like rabbits in burrows for many months. It was a spooky business, and we kept as quiet as mice. I saw or heard nothing to give away the presence of the brigade. Hot tea and burgoo had been prepared and were brought to the assembly in field-kitchens, which was a welcome surprise. Any fears we may have had about being blown to bits in such an exposed position soon faded. Except for a few stray bullets whistling over, nothing disturbed us as we lay on the ground dozing.

The nearest enemy trench was about five hundred yards away, at the top of a slight slope. For a distance of eight miles in a northerly direction, many other brigades of British troops (for this was an all-British show) were similarly massing. There were nearly two thousand pieces of artillery lurking in the rear areas of the attacking front. But the *pièce de résistance* was, of course, the tanks. Like all the rest I was excited at the prospect of going into battle behind these new-fangled Wellsian monsters. I felt they were really going to exact retribution, on behalf of all of us, for the countless miseries and privations that we poor blighters had suffered at Jerry's hands. This was to be the reckoning. The entire Third Army was at the ready, summoned to arms for the great assault.

Zero was at 6.30 am on that memorable day, 20 November. We heard the sound of tank engines warming up. The first glimpse of dawn was beginning to show as we stood waiting for the big bang that would erupt behind us at the end of the count-down. Lieutenant Garbutt and Sergeant Critcher were standing near me. At last the officer began to count. He was bang on, and in a flash the black sky at our backs was ablaze with stabbing shafts of light. A vast drum of terrible thunder swept along the eight-mile front and a chorus of shells screamed over to the east. The need for silence was over, and we exploded in a babble of excitement. That concentration of artillery was surely one of the greatest ever known. The tanks, looking like giant toads, became visible against the skyline as they approached the top of the slope. Some of the leading tanks carried huge bundles of tightly-bound brushwood, which they dropped when a wide trench was encountered, thus providing a firm base to cross over. Suddenly the bombardment ceased. By now the tanks were near the German lines and shooting it out where resistance was met.

The 37th Brigade began to move forward at zero plus one hour in the following order: 7th East Surreys, 6th Buffs, 6th West Kents and 6th Queen's, all in artillery formation. It was a stirring sight, and it was pretty marvellous to know that for one precious hour the tanks had borne the brunt of the attack, and not us. We went forward into enemy country in a manner never possible without the aid of tanks. 'A' Section fell in behind the Queen's, my two guns being on the right flank. No enemy fire of any sort impeded us until we passed Gonnelieu on our left, when we came under a little shell-fire, but suffered no casualties. It was broad daylight as we crossed No Man's Land and the German front line. I saw very few wounded coming back, and only a handful of prisoners. The tanks appeared to have busted through any resistance. The enemy wire had been dragged about like old curtains, though it was not comparable in density to the terrible wire at the beginning of the Somme battle.

I saw two Jerry machine guns which had been put out of action and the gunners finished off. They must have had the shock of their lives pouring their fire into a tank, only to realise that the bullets were bouncing off as the monster lurched towards them. The battalions began to spread out after reaching the crest of the slope. The Queen's were on the right of the advance, flanked by the St Quentin Canal. As we moved forward the ground sloped slightly down; in the distance, nearly a mile ahead, I could see several tanks rolling forward steadily. There did not appear to be any organised defence against them. Some changed direction to meet isolated spots of resistance, mostly from machine guns. One or two had come to a stand-still, probably with engine trouble, as they did not appear to be damaged by enemy action.

From the general situation it seemed to me that the German infantry had either fled at the apparition of the tanks or had pulled out deliberately, leaving their machine guns to do what they could. On the whole I saw remarkably few Jerries about, dead or alive. The fact that the German High Command had been given fourteen months' warning of the advent of tanks would surely inspire careful planning to ease the blow when a big tank assault appeared imminent. Is it possible that over 400 tanks could assemble near our front line, without Jerry knowing anything about it? It's very doubtful.

Whatever the reason for the feeble resistance, it suited my gun team very nicely, and we moved forward steadily with guns and gear. Officialdom had designated tanks sex-wise, ie those with light cannon were males and those with machine guns were females. This caused the lads to think up some bright expressions when viewing the lumbering monsters, such as, 'Here's an old bitch,' or, 'There goes a bloody great bull.'

The village of la Vacquerie, and Pam Pam and Quennet farms were soon taken with little resistance. Proceeding along a communication trench which ran in the direction of the advance, we reached a point where it cut through the banks of a sunken road. We had to cross the road, but pulled up sharp at the sight of three dead Tommies lying on it. I dashed across the road to where the trench continued—a matter of about ten feet. From a concealed position on my right a Jerry machine gun opened fire. My hair stood on end as the bullets hissed past my back. The gunner was just a trifle too late to get me.

There was a tank nearby beginning to move after a stop. I told one of the crew about the enemy machine gun. 'We'll fix the bastard,' he replied, and slowly the tank shuffled round on its tracks and rolled off in the direction of the hostile gun. Then came a fiery burst as the hapless weapon tried to beat off the tank, the bullets clanging and ricocheting. The teams crossed the road safely, well-bucked at this practical demonstration of a tank in action.

The infantry ahead had deployed; some were combing a wood near la Vacquerie, but general mopping up was yet to come. Hostile machine guns still operated from secret nests undiscovered by the advancing troops. They were an irritating menace, as I was yet to find out. My objective with the two guns under my command was the high ground overlooking the St Quentin Canal where it turned westwards across our front. We reached it just before dark. The distance covered from the starting point was roughly seven kilometres. Cambrai was six kilometres further on. During our advance we had seen no targets worthy of our guns, but on our left, over the brow of the slopes, considerable small-arms fire was going on. We had passed several enemy artillery positions but there were no guns to be seen—additional evidence that Jerry had had an inkling of the attack. Whether it was a different story at other parts of the front I, of course, have no knowledge.

Having selected positions for my two guns, we set about digging emplacements and preparing for any counter-attack that might come in the night. Later on, the two other gun teams of 'A' Section turned up on our left. The night was quiet. When daylight came I found that I was the senior NCO present, so for a while I had the four guns on my hands. Although I heard nothing concrete, it appeared that some of the officers and sergeants were casualties.

There was a German artillery dugout a little behind the ridge where our guns were; before I investigated it I lobbed a Mills bomb down the steps. I descended and found a dead Jerry at the bottom, but he was cold. There was a large supply of black bread there but we had a nausea about the stuff, and although ravenous we didn't touch it. I was canny about touching anything in case of booby traps. Some choice souvenir could well tempt me to a sticky end. Since our feed of porridge on the night of 19 November we had been on iron rations, which consisted of a tin of bully beef, hard biscuits, meat extract, and a little tea and sugar.

We used the dugout as our headquarters and resting place. We were all fagged out—I hadn't snatched any sleep for two days. The posting of gun sentries had to be maintained and I had to see that this was done. Several times during the day there were sporadic bursts of machine-gun fire, which appeared to come from the rear and made us a bit jumpy. I knew that it might be days before mopping-up operations were properly organised, so we restricted our movements to a minimum. The four gun positions were about 150 yards apart, with clear fields of fire down the slope to the canal, which lay in the valley 350 to 400 yards distant. On the Jerry side of the canal the ground rose more steeply. It was a clear day, and several Jerries were popping about close to the canal on our side, but there were no targets big enough to justify using the guns. I made a nuisance of myself with a Mauser rifle tormenting stray Jerries. One dropped and didn't get up.

The day passed with nothing of importance happening, there being no further development of the break-through. Nightfall came. A German whizz-bang battery near the village of Masnières began shelling our positions, no doubt having spotted us in daylight. The gun flashes seemed very close from across the valley and the sound of the firing clapped in our ears. The shelling continued with increasing accuracy, and I became alarmed that one or more of the Vickers guns might get knocked out. The German battery was in a vulnerable position on the rising ground just across the canal, and it was well within our range. Never before had I visualised an enemy battery as a target but there it was, about 600 yards away. As a protest and for the good of morale, two of the Vickers guns ripped off a belt each at the battery. The nail of fire did the trick and we had no further trouble that night.

Shortly after midnight an officer came from the 6th West Kents on our left, requesting that the officer in charge of machine guns go with him to his CO, Lieutenant-Colonel Dawson. The duty fell to me and I accompanied the officer to battalion HQ. And so, for the first time in my brief military career, I found myself being addressed by a senior officer concerning military matters, and not for behaviour calling for disciplinary action. I had seen Colonel Dawson on several occasions at the head of his battalion on route marches and I knew that he had the reputation of being an heroic commander. He had been decorated with the DSO and at least three bars up to that stage of the war. In his questioning he was kind and considerate to me, a youngster with quite a bit of responsibility for a while. He wanted to know the number and disposition of my guns. I left him assured and satisfied that his right flank was effectively guarded by four Vickers guns.

As I walked back in the darkness along the ridge overlooking the canal, I felt a warm satisfaction that a battalion commander acknowledged the autonomy of the Machine Gun Corps and accepted this without question from one of its very junior personnel. Where the Queen's were I didn't know. I assumed they were somewhere on our right, but no contact was made with them.

30 Like a scarlet arc

Just after dawn I was very pleased to see Lieutenant Garbutt, who had brought a sergeant with him to relieve me. There was little time in which to learn how the rest of the company had fared. It was 22 November and the finger of fate was beginning to point in my direction. The night drizzle had ceased and the weather was bright and clear. At 8 am Lieutenant Garbutt, a lance-corporal and myself were walking back to company HQ, discussing features of the local terrain. We stopped to look at a map and for a few moments remained motionless. Some undiscovered Jerry machine gunner, destined to take a hand in my affairs, pressed a trigger and a hail of bullets clove the air. I fell as a bullet passed clean through the thickest part of my left thigh, severing the femoral artery.

The Jerry gun continued firing as the three of us lay on the ground, the gunner hoping to polish us off. How can I describe my feelings as I lay, the cone of the bullets scything the grass, knowing that I had already caught a packet? The fact that I was a machine gunner myself increased my fears, and for a few paralysing seconds I felt that death was about to claim me. When the gun stopped my two companions bravely got to work. When they ripped open the leg of my trousers a spout of blood curved upwards like a scarlet arc, three feet long and as thick as a pencil, then disappeared into the ground. Fate was kind to me. Had I been alone, my chances of survival would have been very slim. To stop the blood I bunged my thumb on the hole it spouted from. I was aware I had broken the rules which said that wounds should not be touched by hand, but my action stopped the flow like turning off a tap. The lance-corporal rigged up my bootlaces as a tourniquet and lashed it round my thigh above the wound. I was cold and very hungry. Lieutenant Garbutt was comforting and reassuring, which perked me up a little. It seemed certain that the gun that had wounded me was concealed in a wood 300 yards away. The officer promised that the wood would be combed. I have often wondered if he found it possible to attend to the matter, but I doubt it. He had plenty of other problems to cope with a little later on.

A batch of Jerry prisoners came along under escort and the officer arranged for four of them to carry me to the first-aid post near la Vacquerie on a duckboard. There were a few packets of cigarettes in my haversack, and I gave the Jerries a packet each to induce them to carry me gently, as I was afraid of more bleeding. I knew enough about wounds to realise that, although I was not smashed up, careless handling might have serious results.

Before Mr Garbutt bade farewell, he mentioned as if by way of an afterthought that it was a pity I had not been wounded a few hours later, as my promotion to sergeant was to be recorded in company orders that very day. At that particular time I was quite content to be a corporal, provided I got safely away from the battlefield. But many times since, especially when I was demobbed, I have pondered on how the matter of a few hours deprived me of a sergeant's pay and gratuity. I have no doubt that the CO acted with the best of intentions, but obviously he wanted a sergeant immediately. Army regulations must have tied his hands and Mr Garbutt probably realised this. It was unfair to penalise me, but I suppose many others received the same thankless treatment.

Advanced dressing station near Ginchy, 14 September 1916.
Imperial War Museum Q1220

My German bearers plodded on with me. One was considerably shorter than the others, which didn't help matters. Every few minutes they downed me to have a rest, adding to my suspense. The German heavy guns were waking up and several coal-boxes plunged into la Vacquerie. Tanks which had been used in the assault were parked here and there, but there was very little activity going on around them. Nattering away in their own tongue, which was entirely lost on me, the Jerries had nearly carried me to the first-aid post when four shells came tearing over. They put me down and ran for cover in a nearby shell hole. They were still there when two Tommies came by and carried me the last fifty yards.

Within an hour or so I was in a field hospital under canvas. The surgeons did their job in a large marquee. When I came to, I saw a couple of half-inch rubber tubes extending through the bandages round my thigh. The travelling instructions called for Lysol to be squirted through the tubes every two hours. I was a Blighty case without doubt, and in a few hours I was on board the *Western Australia* again, bound for Southampton.

31 Still in the wood

On 29 November, a Thursday, I arrived at Birkenhead Borough Hospital. It was not a fancy place, but after the turmoil of war it seemed as near to heaven as I was likely to get. Britain was still celebrating the victory of the Third Army and the bells of the churches had rung out in praise. At that time the tank thrust was regarded as the first real turn of the tide against German might. Byng's troops were called the 'Byng Boys', a title that caught on like wildfire. As one of them, fresh from the fray, I attracted my little share of attention from the visitors and nursing staff.

The Lysol syringing was continued and for a while I relaxed in comfort; but there was trouble ahead. At lunchtime on Sunday 2 December, when I lay propped up in bed to deal with the welcome contents on my tray, I became aware of a change of sensation in my thigh. Throwing back the clothes I saw that the bandages were drenched in blood. The wound was leaking fast. I yelled out with fearful wind-up. A young nurse rushed across the ward, took one look at the bloody sight and dashed off. With amazing speed she returned with a young Indian doctor. He pressed hard on my groin and the bleeding stopped. The nurse lashed a rubber tourniquet above the wound, leaving me pillowless while the operating theatre was being made ready.

When I came to my senses the following morning my mother and grandmother were sitting beside the bed. There was a basket affair over my leg and I thought the leg had been amputated, but I was soon put at ease on that score. Happy though I was to see my folks I had no inclination to talk. A policeman had informed them that I was on the danger list, and had handed them free rail passes from Croydon to Birkenhead. They stayed for two days, but money was scarce and they had to return home.

The Indian doctor had put a ligature above the hole in the artery, but I was not yet out of the wood. At lunchtime a week later I was in trouble again. The ligature suddenly failed. I was back where I started, only worse. It was the third severe loss of blood in seventeen days. Doctor Dalziel performed the second operation, and the next morning my mother and an aunt were at my bedside. Blood transfusion was not a part of the surgeon's technique in those days. If you ran out of the precious fluid you were a candidate for the mortuary.

I tell of this harrowing experience merely as a record. I had discovered that getting a 'Blighty one' was not always what it was cracked up to be. With six hot-water bottles around my leg, I overheard the doctor say to the nurse, 'Keep this boy warm. If gangrene sets in all my work will go for nothing.' The doctor was an elderly man then, and must have passed on long ago, but I gratefully remember him for the skill and patience that has given me, up to this moment, over fifty years of life.

As I lay recuperating I received a letter from Lieutenant Garbutt dated 8 December 1917, which I still have. Here is an extract: 'Well, after you left we had a very hot time indeed. Luckily "A" Section was in support which was finally the front line, so you see we did some good by holding him up there. The company got 7 guns away out of the 16, and all fought to the last. The officers lost were Messrs Bowett, Davey and McErvel. "C" and "D" Sections were cut to bits and are about 9 strong each. "A" lost Streeter (missing) and Wilkinson. Keyes, Ashford, Baynes and Dowler wounded.' The letter ends, 'Buck up, get better and hurry back.'

It was very good of Mr Garbutt to spare a moment to write. Although I was as weak as a kitten at the time, his letter made me think that perhaps, later on, if I recovered, I might have to go back. If I had to have another smack, then let it be serving under Lieutenant Garbutt. The news of the Cambrai debacle was a great shock to me. In a few days a classic victory was turned into a wretched defeat, leaving the British people dismayed. I remembered one Tommy in my ward saying, 'What price the "Byng Boys" now? And those bloody bells.' Coming as it did after a year of laboured fighting, the initial and historic success in which I had taken part had fizzled out like a damp squib. Seizing his chance and without tanks, Ludendorff had driven the Third Army back on its heels, capturing a good deal more ground than he had lost ten days earlier.

It soon became evident that our success with the tanks had not been backed up by the necessary reserves to consolidate our gains. The fact is there were not enough troops available as reinforcements. It is my personal opinion that many thousands who would otherwise have been available had been sacrificed uselessly against the barbed wire on the Somme. El Alamein would never have been fought if Monty had not been satisfied that he had sufficient reserves.

32 Recovery and after

On 26 January 1918, my twentieth birthday, I lay in bed opening letters from my relatives and realised how lucky I was to be alive. My uncle, A E Coppard, sent me four pounds, a hefty sum then. I had never possessed such wealth before. There was a censored letter from France, signed on the envelope by Lieutenant Garbutt. This is what it said:

> Dear Coppard   13/1/1918
> Herewith I have great pleasure in enclosing your Soup Ticket. I have also great pleasure in informing you that you have been awarded the Military Medal. Please accept my heartiest congratulations, also Mr Cattell's. Trusting you are progressing favourably and will soon be able to rejoin us.
>
> (Signed W D Garbutt)

The Soup Ticket was a blue linen card, which said:

> Your Commanding Officer and Brigade Commander have informed me that you have distinguished yourself by your conduct in the field.
> I have read their report with much pleasure.
>
> (Signed) A B Scott
> Major-General
> Commanding 12th Division

I took my first walk along the ward in March. I remember going to a window and looking out. There was a row of houses across the street and in one of them a children's party was going on. In the glow of the fire I could see the kiddies playing blind-man's-buff, a heart-warming scene. Time passed, and I was able to enjoy some of the treats laid on by the good people of Birkenhead and Liverpool. The theatres reserved two front rows for the boys in blue, and several parties were held in the Cunard Building. Miss Dorothy Ward, the celebrated comedienne, was the star at one of them and she kissed all of us in the front row. Two or three times a week visitors and welfare people came to the hospital, bringing gifts of all sorts for the patients including home-made cakes, fruit, confectionery and games of various kinds. We often sang hymns together. One kind old lady brought a supply of coloured silks and canvas, and instructed us in the art of embroidery. A sampler which I produced under her guidance so pleased her that she had it framed for me. The billiard parlour of a large private house in Birkenhead was open to us at any time of the day. The maid would bring in morning coffee or afternoon tea with loads of eats. And so it went on.

At the end of June I was discharged from hospital and after sick leave I joined the Machine Gun Corps convalescent camp at Alnwick, Northumberland. Spanish flu struck the camp and caused a setback. Half the troops were laid out in isolation marquees. The only treatment was gargling twice a day. Rumours were current that tens of thousands of people in Spain and other countries had died from that particular brand of flu. It was said that the death roll from it was greater than all the war casualties put together. Lying with others in a cold marquee was not my idea of inducing recovery, and the possibility of snuffing it from any kind of flu, after what I had been through, was disquieting, to say the least.

Sir John Maxwell, GOC Northern Command, came to Alnwick to present medals and I received my Military Medal. The presentation ceremony, which was held before a turn-out of the entire camp, was an exciting experience. The citation in my case read: 'For conspicuous gallantry while in action at Cambrai.' As was the custom at that time, the award of the medal was published in the London Gazette, on 3 March 1918. There was no bounty given with the medal, but recipients in the 1939–45 war collected ten pounds. Why the distinction between the two wars for the same medal? Were the men who first received the medal less deserving of a bounty than those who gained it twenty-odd years later? It would seem that they were.

In due course I was posted back to Harrowby Camp, and for a

while I developed lofty ambitions of obtaining a commission. I
even secured a recommendation from Major H B Wilkins, who
at one time was second-in-command of the 37th Machine Gun
Company. The thing fell though. I was still in medical category
'B'.

It seems I am approaching the end of my story. The great
battle in France was drawing to a close. I have always regretted
that I was not in at the finish of the fighting. To have celebrated
survival with those left of my old company would have been a
privilege indeed. I must record that on Armistice Day the
NAAFI turned up trumps and served free beer all day long,
with no limit.

33 The pay-off

I will not dally any longer. I was demobbed a few days after my
twenty-first birthday, after four and a half years of service. My
leg had shrunk a bit and I was given a pension of twenty-five
shillings per week for six months. The pension dropped to nine
shillings per week for a year and then ceased altogether. At my
last medical board in 1920, one of the members, repeating my
replies to questions, drawled, 'Says femoral artery has been
severed.'

As a corporal I received about twenty-eight pounds as a
gratuity, paid in four separate instalments. A private with
similar service picked up twenty pounds I believe. Demobbed
men were allowed to keep their army overcoats, but if they
didn't want them they could hand them in at any railway station,
for which they received one pound. Overcoats were not cheap
then, and some men kept and wore them for years. The idea of
an army overcoat on top of civvy clothes didn't appeal to me, and
I traded mine in for the quid. It took all my gratuity to clothe me
into something resembling a civilian.

The youth had become a man but with only the capabilities of
a youth to meet adult realities in civvy street. Although an expert
machine gunner, I was a numbskull so far as any trade or craft
was concerned. Lloyd George and company had been full of big
talk about making the country fit for heroes to live in, but it was
just so much hot air. No practical steps were taken to rehabilitate

the broad mass of demobbed men, and I joined the queues for jobs as messengers, window cleaners and scullions. It was a complete let-down for thousands like me, and for some young officers too. It was a common sight in London to see ex-officers with barrel organs, endeavouring to earn a living as beggars. Single men picked up twenty-nine shillings per week unemployment pay as a special concession, but there were no jobs for the 'heroes' who haunted the billiard halls as I did. The government never kept their promise. It is a sad story.

During this time the government, in the flush of victory, were busily engaged in fixing the enormous sums to be voted as gratuities to the high-ranking officers who had won the war for them. Heading the formidable list were Field Marshal Sir Douglas Haig and Admiral Sir David Beatty. For doing the jobs for which they were paid, each received a tax-free golden handshake of £100,000 (a colossal sum then), an earldom and, I believe, an estate to go with it. Many thousands of pounds went to leaders lower down the scale. Sir Julian Byng picked up a trifling £30,000 and was made a viscount. If any reader should ask, 'What did the demobbed Tommy think about all this?' I can only say, 'Well, what do *you* think?'

As I look back and consider the rehabilitation schemes for demobbed men after the 1939–45 war, who received a living wage during months of training for new vocations, with the promise of employment to follow, I realise that we Tommies of the 1914–18 war prepared the way to make life better for those who came after.

In ending this narrative I feel compelled to refer again to the remarkable though brief existence of the Machine Gun Corps. No military pomp attended its birth or decease. It was not a famous regiment with glamour and whatnot, but a great fighting corps, born for war only and not for parades. From the moment of its formation it was kicking. It is with much sadness that I recall its disbandment in 1922; like old soldiers it simply faded away. There is a fine statue at Hyde Park Corner erected in memory of the corps, called 'The Boy David', by Derwent Wood, RA. The inscription on it reads:

> Saul hath slain his thousands,
> But David his tens of thousands.

The Boy David by Derwent Wood, RA: the Machine Gun Corps Memorial at Hyde Park Corner. *Imperial War Museum MH24461*

An Old Comrades Association still exists and its members meet annually at the memorial.

Very soon now, the last survivor of the 1914–18 war will have faded away. Those of us who are still going strong are surely deeply thankful to Providence for having been spared. Just recently I have discovered that an old 12th Division man lives close to me and my heart leaps when I spot him walking up the road. We never miss a natter, and his eyes shine as we go over the umpteenth episode of our war experiences. We catch vivid memories of the past and are glad that we were young in 1914.

> Today's my daughter's wedding day,
> Fifty thousand pounds I'll give away.
> Hooray! Hooray!

Epilogue: **Brief glimmer of youth**

I am on board the MV *Invicta* at Dover, and it's just moving off, bound for Calais. It is Sunday 5 June 1972 and there are not very many people travelling. The second-class bar is open, displaying an attractive selection of duty-free goods, and I buy a carton of cigarettes and a bottle of cognac. Unscrewing the bottle-top, I take a small swig now and then which makes me feel good, for I'm off to the Flanders battlefields: to Ypres, Ploegsteert, Loos, the Somme, Arras and Cambrai.

I confess I'm just a little excited, as it is fifty-seven years almost to the day since I was on board a much cruder *Invicta*, a coal burner, that carried the officers and men of the 6th Battalion, The Queen's Royal West Surrey Regiment. I certainly should go down on my knees and thank Providence for permitting me to live long enough to be able to make this journey. For a few days I will quietly forget my wife, bless her, our two daughters, three grandchildren, even Britain itself, with its strikes and confused way of life, and I'll be thinking of my old comrades who shared the dangers, privations and miseries of trench life so long ago.

It is a fact that with one exception, until my book was published, I had not met a single soul who served in the 6th Queen's, and since then I have met two only. The exception was a strange encounter that occurred in the early thirties when I was a Customs officer at Newhaven. I was behind the baggage benches assisting in the examination of passengers' baggage and effects. Over twelve hundred travellers were swarming off the ship, and the Customs staff were hard at work obtaining satisfactory declarations from them as they sought to get clearance, if possible without having to open their baggage.

My memory for faces has always been pretty reliable and, glancing up at an elderly gentleman accompanied by his wife and children, I recognised my old CO. 'Now here's a chance to settle some of the old scores,' I said to myself. 'This is the fellow who gave me a fearful dressing-down and seven days' confined to barracks when I overstayed my final leave before going overseas.' For one mean moment I contemplated the pleasure I would get by giving the colonel's baggage the full treatment, but discretion prevailed, and I gave him speedy clearance. Before his departure I made myself known to him, but I was somewhat annoyed that he didn't seem to remember me at all, although I served in his battalion for fourteen months.

The ship is nearing Calais. After a short train journey to Hazebrouck, I expect to be greeted by my Belgian pen-friend Leopold, whom I have not yet had the pleasure of meeting. He came across my book in the library of St George's Memorial Church, Ypres, and wrote to me. In his last letter he said, 'I am short and will have my little nephew with me.' I replied, 'I am old and wear a deaf-aid in my right ear.' As well as inviting me to Belgium, he had arranged for me to stay at Talbot House (Toc H) in Poperinge, well known as a historic meeting place for old soldiers of the Great War who wish to tour the battlefields.

As I wait for the train to depart for Hazebrouck, my mind goes back to 1 June 1915. On that day I travelled with my battalion, eleven hundred strong, packed in cattle-trucks. We arrived at St Omer at night. The train stopped at a siding and orders were given to disembark. A corporal who apparently had a smattering of French asked a railwayman where we were. The answer must have baffled the corporal, who kept silent. 'What did the bloke say?' yelled several chaps, and the reply came, 'Blimey, I dunno. Sounded like "Cetewayo" to me.' Screams of laughter followed. Cetewayo, the Zulu king, had a name that was not unknown to some of us. He cropped up occasionally in history lessons at school, as he was captured and brought to England in 1877.

I arrive at Hazebrouck Station and meet Leopold at the exit. There is no mistaking him: a short, stocky man, with a young child. My head whirls as my friend pours out a torrent of English in a strident voice with an unfamiliar accent that rattles my hearing-aid. I tone it down a bit and I hear him a little better, but unfortunately his car has a left-hand drive, so I must sit on his right side, which is not so good for my hearing.

Leopold is a very fast driver, covering the twenty kilometres to Poperinge quickly. We enter Talbot House, one of the grand old town houses which were practically untouched by the war. Madame Lucienne Lamond, the manageress, lives here with Tony, her husband, and their four children. She shows me round the lofty rooms: the walls are covered with well-preserved caricatures, poems, mementoes and photographs, contributed by officers and other ranks, many of whom were killed in the Ypres salient. The large whitewashed loft is a consecrated chapel, rigged up hastily by troops in December 1915. The altar is formed by a carpenter's bench found in an old shed at the bottom of the garden. It is covered by a rich altar cloth, the gift of Guards officers in memory of their comrades who died in 1916. Lucienne, a pretty Belgian blonde with blue eyes, tells me that many soldiers were baptised in this chapel before returning to the trenches. There is much to see in the fine old house, and I must take it all in during my stay.

My companion reminds me that it is 5.30 pm. I want him to take me to evensong at St George's Memorial Church, Ypres. We leave and get to Ypres in twenty minutes. It is said that this church and the British Settlement owe their origin to an urgent appeal by Field Marshal Earl French for a memorial to the half-million soldiers whose remains lie in the garden of Flanders and in silent cities. During the Second World War the church was used as a place of worship by the German forces. Leopold says that during the occupation by the Germans they borrowed a stove and the chairs; they promised to return them to the church, but failed to bring back the stove. The church is situated within a stone's throw of the Cloth Hall and St Martin's Cathedral, both magnificent examples of Belgian restoration skills.

Much to my pleasure, Leopold reveals that he possesses a splendid tenor voice, and he uses it in no uncertain manner, showing a fine understanding of the form of the Church of England service. The walls of the church are covered with brass plaques, all highly polished, in memory of many famous regiments, and I feel a glow of satisfaction when I observe one commemorating the Machine Gun Corps. In this corps of 170,000 officers and other ranks, 13,791 were killed, and 48,258 wounded or missing. Reflecting on the size of these figures, I speculate on the probability that where a man was a casualty more than once, as in my case, his wounding would also be recorded more than once. Leopold scans the church library and shows me the copy of my book which caused him to write to me; he is pleased to know that I have a copy for him in my bag at Toc

H. We leave St George's Church and in a few steps enter St Martin's Cathedral, which is separated from the great Cloth Hall by a kind of courtyard. Although it has taken over fifty years to restore these immense constructions from a vast amount of rubble, it is amazing when one considers what a mighty task it must have been to clear the city before rebuilding could start. In the cathedral I notice a highly decorative plaque dedicated to

The glory of God and to the memory of one million dead of the British Empire who fell in the Great War, many of whom rest in Belgium.

The illuminated arms of Great Britain, Northern Ireland, India, New Zealand, Australia, South Africa and Canada form part of the display on the plaque. In this great cathedral are several statues of saints, which did not escape severe damage by shelling and falling masonry. Mutilated, they make a pathetic sight: one has lost its hands and half its head. Four recumbent figures lie on massive marble bases, all of them similarly damaged, a reminder of the Great War for generations to come. King Albert I of Belgium is commemorated by the rose window in the west transept given by the British Army and the Royal Air Force.

At 7.55 pm Leopold and I stand at the Menin Gate in readiness for the ceremony of the Last Post. The arch-like memorial stretches across the road, from one side to the other. It is familiar to thousands of Britishers, and the names of 55,000 British soldiers who have no known graves are inscribed on its walls. At 7.58 pm traffic ceases to pass under the great arch, and all approaches near the memorial are suddenly silent. As if by magic, the whole of this ancient city is suddenly still. With many others we stand under the arch, and at 8 pm we hear the faultless rendering of the Last Post by two uniformed Belgian trumpeters. As the last notes die away I'm practically in tears. This daily homage to the dead, carried on by the Belgians for many years now, is surely the most emotional expression of the sorrow of the world ever conceived. None, except those with hearts of stone, can remain unmoved.

Leopold takes me back to Poperinge and promises to call for me tomorrow. What a fine chap he is. Nothing is too much trouble for him to explain, and he seems to know the answer to

The Menin Gate, Ypres.   *Commonwealth War Graves Commission*

everything. I'm certain that my next few days with him will be a complete success. At the end of this long day I feel worn out.

It is a bright new day, and Leopold calls for me from his home in the country about fifteen kilometres from Poperinge. He is to attend a business conference at Tourcoing, a large French town just over the frontier. I understand it is something to do with the passage of goods crossing the frontier both ways, at Halluin, a check-point where Common Market procedure controls all traffic. On our way to Tourcoing we turn off the main road from the Menin Gate. We drive up a superb avenue of maple trees and come to the Canadian War Memorial near Sanctuary Wood. This memorial takes the form of massive stone terracing rising from a noble black marble frontage, its lettering deeply incised. In the cemetery close by is the grave of Lieutenant Gilbert Talbot of the Rifle Brigade, killed in 1915, in whose memory Talbot House is named. As we move away we pass a bizarre outdoor museum containing specimens of rusty war gear. Steel helmets torn by shrapnel and stuck on weapons impaled in the ground do not make a pretty sight. I am reminded of Alexander the Great, who, before leaving India, caused a number of specially-made outsize weapons, mangers and bridles to be left there, casually scattered about, in order to exaggerate his glory to posterity. I'm afraid posterity will derive no feeling of glory from gazing at the rusting and uninspiring collection displayed there.

Sitting in the sun at Tourcoing while Leopold is attending the conference, I ponder on the amazing development of the organisation of Toc H, born in Talbot House, and how it has developed from a refuge for weary soldiers in the war. Originally founded by Neville Talbot (brother of Gilbert) and the Reverend Tubby Clayton, both padres in the 6th Division, it is today a world-wide concern of 20,000 volunteers who work to ease suffering in depressed areas throughout the world.

The conference over, my companion joins me, and we drive via Armentières to le Touquet, just inside the frontier on the Belgian side. By this time I have grasped the fact that my friend is a very capable and enthusiastic amateur researcher of the history of the Great War, especially of events that occurred near the Franco-Belgian border. I am grateful that his knowledge of English is so good, as he talks incessantly. I try hard to keep up with him but it is not easy.

A chapter in my book is of special interest to him, and he wishes me to retrace my steps over the ground where the 6th Battalion, The Queen's, took over the le Touquet trenches from Princess Patricia's Light Infantry Regiment of Canada in June 1915. As elsewhere, after over half-a-century, the area around le Touquet and the neighbouring village of le Bizet, has completely changed, or so it seems. New roads, the disappearance of old houses and the ribbon development of new houses disguise the whole scene for me. The skylines too have changed, owing to the growth of new trees. But Leopold is indefatigable in his efforts to trace any particular place, and he ferrets out information like a first-class detective, speaking French, Belgian and German, apparently with equal facility. He presents a most cordial approach to those whom he is questioning, and always gets a friendly and helpful response.

Our present purpose is to locate an avenue of trees in this neighbourhood, to ascertain if they were planted in place of those the German artillery were continually shattering in 1915, during the period the Queen's were here. Following local enquiries we succeed in finding the avenue, but the trees are not fully grown. They have not the girth or height of those I remember. We enter the avenue. On the left is a large British cemetery where New Zealanders were interred—during 1917 only. Leopold mentions that it is useless to search in this cemetery for the graves of Sergeant-Major W Annis and two of my companions who were killed in the le Touquet trenches in the summer of 1915. As we move along the avenue I look out for farm buildings on the left, but for a while the tree trunks obscure the view, as the buildings are set back a little from the roadside. I begin to think that it is highly probable that they do not exist any more, but at last the walls of red-brick buildings begin to come into view. As we draw abreast of them my doubts disappear. I know this place like the back of my hand, for it is where No. 13 Platoon of my regiment was billeted when in reserve. How could I forget the night I was on sentry-go in this avenue, with my back to the wall of the barn in which the platoon was sleeping?

We enter the farmyard to talk to the occupants of the farmhouse, but they are not at home. I spot a crucifix standing where I remember the old one had been. It is made of iron and the figure of Christ is enamelled white. A French workman appears and Leopold questions him; obtaining promising information, we set off to an address in le Touquet. A very old lady there tells us that her husband is probably playing cards with some of his cronies at an estaminet about two kilometres away. The chase continues, and at the estaminet (which is situated on the very edge of the frontier) M Devroede, a gentleman of eighty-four, steps forward from a group of elderly men in answer to Leopold's enquiry. 'Yes,' he says, 'my brother was tenant there, at the farm in the avenue during the Great War. Ah, the crucifix. That was a wooden one then. All those big trees were knocked down by German artillery, and later on, during a hard winter, the stumps were sawn down for fuel. New trees were planted and are growing there now,' added the old gentleman. The card players, mostly of the same age as myself, and two or three much older, evince deep interest in the discussion. I smile at them while they give me a good looking over. Leopold tells them I was a British soldier in these parts fifty-seven years ago, which makes them sit up a little. M Devroede calls for some beer and the company drink to my health, which, I must say, I find most pleasing. Actually, I did discover one of the original trees in the avenue, which had escaped destruction, its trunk hidden by very tall undergrowth. Its height exceeds that of its neighbours by a good twenty feet.

We drive to Poperinge through a picturesque landscape of fields and meadows. As is his habit whilst driving, my companion talks rapidly in English, and I do my best to keep up with him. Occasionally he jams on the brakes, grabs a piece of paper and scribbles down something I have said. I must confess that for some of the time my mind drifts away, and I am back in khaki again with my pals. He breaks in, 'We shall go to Bailleul Communal Cemetery tomorrow, to see if we can find the grave of your Company Sergeant-Major Annis.' I think of my old CSM who was killed by a rifle-grenade in July 1915. Leopold carries on, 'Then we'll go to Allouagne to see if we can find Maria, your old sweetheart in 1916, but it won't be easy. She could well be dead by now.'

These remarks of Leopold really set me thinking. Maria had a sister named Marie; if they are both alive they must be in their mid-seventies at least. In any case, why should I assume they are still alive and living in Allouagne now? Tomorrow I will find out, one way or the other. Safely back in Talbot House, Madame Lucienne serves me with three fried eggs and a pile of golden chips, which are marvellous. Worn out, I retire at 10 pm.

★   ★   ★   ★

I sleep for ten hours, and before breakfast I walk in the garden and make the acquaintance of a tortoise named Adam. His name is painted on each side of his shell. As I talk to him he pokes his head out carefully and allows me to stroke it. He certainly seems to appreciate a bit of human conversation. Promptly at 9 am Leopold arrives and we are soon heading for Bailleul Communal

Cemetery. He has contacted the War Graves Commission at Ypres and has obtained the index number of CSM Annis's grave, which we quickly locate. As I stand beside it, I find it difficult to comprehend properly that my old CSM has been in this grave for so many years. Three-quarters of my life have passed away since his death. I well remember how once, when he spoke to me, I stammered a little and he cut in with 'Come on Coppard, spit it out.' But he wasn't a harsh man by any means and the men of 'D' Company had great respect for him. His headstone indicates that he was forty years old when he was killed, and the inscription on it reads, 'Underneath are the Everlasting Arms.' A strange choice, the word 'Underneath', I think. I would not have chosen it myself.

Close by I notice a headstone in memory of

T. MOTTERSHEAD, VC. DCM.

R.F.C. 12–1–17

This cemetery contains well over five thousand graves, mostly British, but there are a few German and American ones. What surprises me most, is forty odd graves where men of the Chinese Labour Corps are buried. During the war I saw very little of the corps, although I knew of its existence. On the headstones, in Chinese characters, is the name of the soldier, followed by an inscription in English, 'A good reputation endureth for ever.' I take it that these words are a translation from a Chinese motto, and I like them very much.

Leopold points out a bronze locker in a wall near the entrance to the cemetery, which contains a register of the dead and a visitors' book, in which I write, 'I came to see the grave of CSM Annis; 6th Batt the Queen's. This cemetery beautifully kept.' This is indeed the truth, and a written compliment is the least that one can do to thank and encourage the gardening staff. The ground is one vast lawn in first-class condition, and there are shrubs of all descriptions in flowering abundance. The miles of lawn edges are trimmed with great skill and accuracy. There are several fine trees here and there in the cemetery, standing on watch as if guarding the sanctity of this holy ground.

Taking leave of a cheery British gardener, we make for le Touret Cemetery, where my friend, complying with a request, checks the details on some of the headstones. He tells me that occasionally he receives enquiries from the United Kingdom.

On our way to Chocques, which I want to visit, we pass through Béthune, a flourishing French town near the mining area, which gave considerable hospitality and comfort to literally thousands of our troops who occupied billets there. The Red Lamp just off the town square used to do a roaring trade.

As we drive through the town I tell Leopold that in October 1915 I deposited a silver wrist-watch for repair at a watch maker's shop near Béthune railway station, and that I had never had the opportunity to call for it. He takes this news seriously, and suggests that we enquire at the Gendarmerie, but I implore him not to think of it; I am very relieved when he agrees that after this lapse of time the chances of success are infinitesimal. We have a good laugh over this.

In 1916, when I was batman to Lieutenant Wilkie, he was hospitalised in the château at Chocques. As he was entitled to the services of his batman I accompanied him to the hospital, thus escaping the horrors of the Hohenzollern Redoubt for a few days. Today, although it is still there and in good repair, the château is not occupied, and is hemmed in by workshops of a sprawling plastics factory.

Now, Leopold is driving me to the village of Allouagne to try and find Maria. It seems strange but I cannot recall a single detail about her sister Marie. The village has grown a bit and become modernised, with new bungalows on the outskirts, and as we drive slowly through it I see nothing that I can remember. Leopold stops beside a party of farm workers at the side of the road and asks the whereabouts of the Bailleul family. They consider the matter carefully, and talk rapidly among themselves, mentioning the name of Maria several times; but in the end they say that they have not heard of the Bailleul family and suggest that I must have got them mixed up with the town of the same name.

In the heart of the village Leopold tackles a man who turns out to be a local functionary of some sort. Apparently he knows everybody. He gives a curious set of directions, with a lot of twisting of fingers and scythe-like sweeping movements of the arms. Seeing my companion's enlightened expression and hearing odd snatches of conversation, it becomes clear to me that this kind gentleman actually knows where Maria lives. Leopold drives to a cross roads where two cafés stand on

opposite corners and makes a U-turn. After a crawl of four
hundred metres or so there it is, a farm frontage with a large
green door in the middle. My interpreter leading, we open the
door and step in. On each side of us are large waggon sheds;
straight ahead across a roomy paved farmyard is the farmhouse
where Madame Veuve Benoit Caron, *née* Maria Bailleul, lives. A
middle-aged man opens the door of the farmhouse and
Leopold, with his usual courteous approach, makes enquiries.
'Yes, Maria is here. This is where she lives,' says the man, as
he invites us into the house. Stepping over the threshold I see
two women; the man, who is Maria's son, points to the elder one
and says, 'That is Maria!' I look at her and see a genteel old lady
neatly dressed in black. It is not difficult for my memory to leap
from youth to old age as I study the lady's face. It is Maria
without doubt, and I note that she still retains much of the good
looks of her youth. Naturally, I am pleased about this, as it is
positive evidence that I must have had discriminating taste
when I was young.

Leopold tells her who I am and her face lights up with
surprise as I step forward to greet her. Placing my hands on her
shoulders I kiss both her cheeks, in which little ceremony she
fully joins. She nods and smiles as her recognition of me
becomes complete. The other lady present is her daughter-in-
law. There is much conversation going on, and Leopold is in his
element, but I do manage to get in a little talk with Maria. She
tells me she is seventy-six. I tell her that I'm seventy-four,
which makes us laugh happily together, with good reason; for
have we not reached the twilight of things, each in our separate
ways, yet both of us able to look back to a few happy hours of our
youth? Opening a copy of *With a Machine Gun to Cambrai*,
Leopold points to a photograph of me taken eighteen months
after I had last seen Maria. He reads aloud the passages where I
mention her; she goes into a spasm of laughter and we all follow
suit. Age does not seem to matter a bit, although Maria does
suffer from arthritis and uses a stick. At Leopold's invitation we
go outside to be photographed. She sits in a chair and hides her
stick, while I stand beside her with my hand on her shoulder. It
is time for celebration, and Maria's son thoughtfully produces
some good wine. Suddenly Maria hurries from the room and
returns with an old notebook, which I recognise as an old British

The author with Maria, June 1972.   *George Coppard*

one of the type used so long ago. On several pages I see some pencilled elementary French phrases and I feel pretty sure that the writing is mine.

It is time to depart, and I am happy that I have been spared to see a good friend of my youth. I am certain that she feels the same. Maria has two sons and two daughters, and has been a widow for sixteen years. Her sister Marie died many years ago.

Later we call on Maria's nephew and his wife at the old farmhouse where I was billeted. I notice that the little bakehouse exists no more, though its foundations are still visible. I calculate that a big puddle marks the exact spot where I used to sleep. Although the buildings surrounding the farmyard are much the same as years ago, I see no waggon wheels lying about: empty oil drums and old tyres take their place and the pleasant aroma of farm manure is drowned by the fumes of hydrocarbon oils. Not a welcome change, I think.

★   ★   ★   ★

We proceed to Vermelles, and I recall that Major-General F D V Wing, CB, CMG, commanding the 12th Division was killed on the Vermelles-Hulluch road near this spot on 2 October 1915. I examine the register in the Vermelles Cemetery, but the general's name is not there. Leopold says he will get the details from the War Graves Commission. We are now on the fringe of the Loos battlefield; several houses of the town's development scheme actually encroach upon it. In Vermelles itself I see no trace of the old and famous brewery whose vaults provided so much warmth and comfort and not a little protection to troops coming from the trenches for a rest. I remember some uproarious games of Brag, Pontoon, and Crown and Anchor in the safety of the deep vaults.

Passing through Vermelles, we climb in an easterly direction, up a slight gradient towards Hulluch. On either side of us are broad stretches of cultivated land, running from Auchy-les-Mines on the left, to Loos on the right, a distance of about six kilometres. Fields of corn and other crops bend gracefully in the gentle wind. On this very land, pock-marked by thousands of German shell holes, Britain suffered sixty thousand casualties in the great battle that lasted a month. Deep communicating trenches stretched from the Vermelles area, up the slope to various points in the front line near the top; the actual summit, as was nearly always the case, was held by the enemy. Troops were continually moving to and from the front line via the communicating trenches, one of which was later called Wing's Way. Everywhere on this battlefield lay wrecked weapons of war, dead horses and limbers. The Allied objective was the mining town of Lens, but the combined British and French forces failed to capture it.

As I gaze across the rich hedgeless fields I find it hard to believe that when I was seventeen I actually took part, as a Vickers machine gunner, in that bloody battle. I soon come across evidence of the battle as we drive up to the top of the hill, for there are the iron gates of St Mary's Cemetery on the right of the road. This burial ground is close to where the old British front line was situated before the attack, and I am not surprised on entering to discover the headstones of many men of the Black Watch and other famous Highland Regiments as well as the Guards Division. On 29 September 1915 I had seen many of their bodies as they lay in hundreds in front of the German barbed wire as far as Loos, three to four kilometres from this cemetery. We sign the visitors' book and turn sadly away.

*   *   *   *

We move on, and I begin to notice much evidence of coal-mining and other industrial development close to Hulluch. There is an enormous conical slag heap, new to me; I look left to locate a long slag-heap we Tommies used to call Fosse 8, but I cannot find it. This disturbs me a little and I wonder if my memory is letting me down. There is a housing estate close by and Leopold commences to make enquiries there. We are directed to the house of an 'old' man, who answers the door with his entire family, his wife and five good-looking children. Leopold opines that the man is not very old and probably has little knowledge of the local events of the Great War, but the French householder asserts that he is sixty-one, and we all laugh. He has heard of Fosse 8, which he describes as a pithead at Auchy-les-Mines. But he does not know of a slag-heap of that name. It occurs to me that perhaps we Tommies had been in error in giving the name of the mine itself to its slag-heap. Anyway, the slag-heap has clearly vanished.

Our final question to the French householder concerns the
position of the Hohenzollern Redoubt, but a shake of the head
indicates that he has never even heard of it. This is strange
indeed, yet perhaps it is as well that the gentleman does not
know that the redoubt was a small Ypres, where thousands of
British soldiers died a short distance from where he now lives
with his family; that it formed the left flank of the Loos battle
where the enemy would not yield; that the fighting went on for
three and a half years without any significant gain either by the
Germans or ourselves; that it took the form of giant mine craters
that fused both front lines together; that men fought to gain
possession of a newly-made crater almost before the last lumps
of hundreds of tons of earth and rock blasted sky-high had
dropped to the ground; and that one day in October 1918 word
travelled swiftly along the trenches near the redoubt, 'Jerry's
gone.' It all happened a long time ago and the Frenchman with
his family lives in peace.

Where is the Hohenzollern Redoubt? Where are the ten great
holes, each of which required over 50,000 pounds of ammonal to
produce? What about the hundreds of thousands of tons of coal
slag in that elongated monster I knew as Fosse 8? Leopold says,
'Let's go to Auchy-les-Mines. Someone there will surely provide
the answer.' So we make our way there, and after some enquiries
arrive at a house where lives an old French soldier who fought at
Verdun. We find the old fellow sitting on his doorstep in the sun.
He tells us that he is eighty-four years old and proudly bares his
left arm, which we see is horribly mutilated—'By shrapnel at
Verdun,' he informs us. He only has limited use of the limb, but he
tells us that this is better than having it lopped off. He has a fresh
complexion and bright blue eyes and is a very lively little man in
all respects. He offers to enlighten us about the Fosse 8 slag heaps.
He also knows about the big craters, but doesn't realise they were
called the Hohenzollern Redoubt, as the French army never
fought there. He gets in the car with us. Just before we move off,
three stout young men emerge from the house and want to know
where we are taking their grandfather. The Verdun veteran
assures them that there is nothing to worry about, and Leopold
explains that I once fought in these parts and want to look around
the battlefield.

We trundle along a rough track until, clear of the mining

precincts, we emerge into open country. We are now looking back towards Hulluch. Soon we get out and help the old man to climb a grassy bank. On the top is a very rough wide area stretching a kilometre or more, scarcely supporting the growth of a few weeds. On the ground at my feet I see no soil, only waste slag; here and there are large lumps of black rock. Crops on both sides of this barren land move gently with the breeze as we walk slowly with the old guide, who opens our eyes as he tells his tale. Having already formed a suspicion in my mind, I do not require much convincing that we are actually standing on the land where Fosse 8 once was, and that its vast bulk has long since been used to fill up the craters of the Hohenzollern Redoubt.

From where I stand, I judge that the former site of the Hohenzollern Redoubt is about a kilometre away and that it probably covered three or four acres. At one time the craters there were, on average, thirty to thirty-five feet deep and a hundred to a hundred and twenty feet across the rim. Terrible and sustained fighting went on merely to capture these great holes, some of which overlapped each other. The whole business was stupid and futile.

The Verdun veteran tells us that after the war had ended a big first-aid post was found inside the back of the Fosse, as well as storerooms and tunnels leading to defence positions camouflaged on the face of it. I feel a grim satisfaction that I can verify with my own eyes that the thing is well and truly spread-eagled, and will never rise again. We express our gratitude to the old soldier for showing and explaining so much that we wanted to know and deliver him safely to his grandsons.

On the way back to Poperinge my thoughts turn to my old war comrade, Lance-Corporal William Hankin, who was Number One of the Vickers gun team in the Hohenzollern Redoubt. I have often pictured him through the passing years, and I am happy to say that I always remember him as he was when I was his Number Two and shared his enthusiasm for maintaining the efficiency of our Vickers gun. I see a sturdy and very strong man of twenty years, possessing much manly vigour and individual personality. His coolness under the intense fire we had to endure in the redoubt was always a wonder to me and helped me to control my fears.

I sleep like a log and awake to another lovely day. I have

breakfast with a padre, two ladies and a gentleman. They have come from Toc H Headquarters in London to attend the funeral of a Belgian lady who had for many years been closely connected with the work of Toc H in Belgium. They leave to attend the funeral. Very soon I hear the mournful tolling of a church bell and I am drawn into the street. There are many people walking in the same direction; following them, I arrive at the church at the same time as the funeral cortège. Eight young ladies walk beside the hearse. They are dressed in dark blue attire, with black lace head-dresses which trail to their shoulders. The coffin is of ebony with silver fixtures, and the hearse is extremely decorative in a funereal manner. The whole affair is most sumptuous and dignified. I notice two immense wreaths, one from Toc H and the other from a similar organisation in Berlin. Two of the church attendants are receiving cards from people entering the church. Apparently anyone can go in, but they must complete a card first. Several people are filling in cards, but never having seen this procedure before I find it a little puzzling. I presume the bereaved mourners wish to know the style and title of people who attend the funeral service.

I saunter round this fine little town of Poperinge. For the cleanliness of its streets and the high tone of its many small shops it deserves a gold medal. Neither a match nor a cigarette-end do I see lying about. Turning a corner I notice a little old man sweeping the pavement in front of a café. I am about to pass by him when, without any hesitation, he speaks to me in good English and in a few minutes tells me his life story, a most unusual one I must say.

On leaving school soon after the Great War he got a job with a British Burial Section of the War Graves Commission and was continuously employed by them for fifty-three years. The section was principally concerned with recovering the remains of dead soldiers found in the battle areas and burying them in cemeteries suitable to their nationality, if that was possible. He tells me that the separation of German from British dead was, more often than not, decided by the colour of the bones of the skeleton, especially if supported by even the smallest fragment of uniform. He is quite serious as he explains that German bones are decidedly greyish in colour and British ones white. When I enquire about the colour of French and Belgian bones he replies that the areas that he worked in throughout the years always seemed to be where the British and Germans fought each other.

Leopold will be calling for me at about 1 pm, so this is a good opportunity for me to browse around Talbot House. I climb the steep stairs to the loft, which houses the immaculately whitewashed chapel. The first thing that catches my eye is a miniature font, six inches square and six inches high, an exquisite model of the richly ornamented font in Winchester Cathedral. As an infant the Reverend Tubby Clayton was baptised in this little font in Queensland, Australia, and it was used to baptise many fighting men before they returned to the front. It stands securely on a fine mahogany plinth about three feet high. A small brass plate is affixed to it, which reads:

In memory of Lt. G. William Morris,
8th, K.O.Y.L.I.
From a brother officer

There is also a carved wooden chair, the back of which unfolds to form a table top. A brass plate on it reads:

To the Glory of God and in memory of
L/Cpl Archie Forrest
P. Special Coy, R.E.
Baptised and confirmed in this chapel
Killed in action, 1917.

The chair is called the confirmation chair and it has been used by the Archbishop of Canterbury for this purpose. Also in the chapel is a very beautiful picture in sepia tones of Christ giving the Blessed Sacrament. It cost only ten shillings, being part of a much larger sum donated in memory of

Edmund Street, D.S.O.
Major 2nd Sherwoods
Killed September, 1916,
On the Somme.

The heart of Toc H is the Chaplain's Room, furnished and maintained today exactly as it was sixty years ago; from here the Reverend Tubby Clayton ran his haven of peace.

In one of the rooms I notice a postcard in a frame, on which is written the famous verse, 'They shall not grow old as we that are left grow old.' The card was purchased in an auction room, and the author of the verse, Lawrence Binyon, certifies that his signature on the card is genuine.

I am touched as I see all round me in this lovely old house much evidence of the Christian way of life yet, as I look back to my time in the trenches, I do not remember that any of us youngsters, or even older men, discussed religion. As a topic it just didn't exist. But I acknowledge the debt that weary soldiers owed to such a place as Talbot House, where warmth, food and comfort were ungrudgingly given, and I can recall many happy hours spent at odd times in church canteens. I don't know what we would have done without them. As I move around this old house, admiring the cartoons and sketches done by soldiers of long ago, I reflect how fortunate I am that my return to the battlefields should be, as it were, under the wing of Toc H. This place has a kind of parental welcome about it and I find it easy to sink into memories of my youth.

The humour of the Reverend Tubby Clayton is clearly shown by notices in large print affixed to various parts of Talbot House. In the hall is a notice which reads:

> *If you are in the habit of spitting on the carpet at home, please do so here.*
> *By Order   P.B.C.*

Another reads:

> *The waste paper baskets are purely ornamental*
> *By Order   P.B.C.*

At the top of a flight of steep stairs is the following notice:

> *No Amy Robsart stunts down these stairs*
> *By Request   P.B.C.*

And on a wall near the entrance:

> *To pessimists ———⟶ Way Out*

Another, and more formal notice, illuminated and probably hand-painted, gives the *Roll of Honour of the British Empire* throughout the First World War. I find this most moving, reflecting as it does the response of almost all parts of the empire, great and small, to meet a common enemy.

BRITISH EMPIRE
ROLL OF HONOUR

ROYAL NAVY

Personnel August 15th, 1914	147,667
Total enlistments 1914–1918	407,316

THE BRITISH ARMY

Personnel August 1st, 1914   733,514
Enlistments 1914–1918:

England	3,987,804	Canada	619,636
Scotland	557,618	Australia	416,809
Wales	272,924	New Zealand	124,211
Ireland	133,902	Fiji	680
Isle of Man	8,261	Malay States	2,303
Jersey	5,748	India	1,338,620
Guernsey		Ceylon	2,182
Alderney	4,915	South Africa	136,074
Sark		Rhodesia	5,200
Newfoundland	9,826	East Africa	26,300
Bermuda	360	Nyasaland	10,800
West Indies		Gold Coast	10,287
British Guiana	15,950	Nigeria	15,567
British Honduras		Sierra Leone	694
Malta	3,000	Gambia	371
Cyprus	3,000		

Total Enlistments 1914–1918   7,712,772

ROYAL AIR FORCE

Personnel 1914	1,900
Total enlistments 1914–1918	293,522

Grand total of men who served in the Navy, Army and Air Force
from August 1914 to November 1918   9,296,691
Died for The Empire   1,066,468

＊   ＊   ＊   ＊

Leopold arrives on time, and we drive northwards to Westvle-
teren, which, he says, has some very good beer, brewed in the
local monastery of Saint Sixtus and sold in the estaminet
opposite the monastery gates. The manageress speaks fluent
English and explains that the estaminet is owned by the

monastery. The beer is as dark as Guinness, but tastes like a mixture of beer and wine with plenty of body in it, which I notice as soon as I get on my feet to depart. It is served in large stemmed glasses, ornamentally stamped 'St Sixtus Abbey', but they are strictly not for sale, as I found out when I tried to purchase one. There is no doubt that the beer is excellent and powerful—which it should be at twenty-eight pence per quarter-litre. During the Second World War the Germans were very fond of this beer, and the licensing hours had to be reduced to two hours a day. The manageress mentioned that, for a time, the baggage of Field-Marshal Montgomery was kept in the care of the estaminet. A St Sixtus monk is on duty at the monastery gate, but we are not permitted to enter the brewery unless purchasing beer commercially.

In the Langemark area we visit a very large German cemetery. The broad stone entrance has a massive severity about it, typically German, which reminds me of their solid blockhouses; this prepares one for what lies through its dark portals. There are no headstones here, as in British and most French cemeteries. Instead, on a vast lawn of fine grass, are hundreds of stone tablets, lying flat, each one with the names and rank of twenty German soldiers who are buried beneath. Perfectly level, and each resting on a foundation of concrete to prevent subsidence, the tablets, with the grass between them, cause the cemetery to look like a huge chequer board, the flat pieces lying in relief. From a vantage point one sees the whole cemetery with the lines of tablets, rigidly precise and accurate, whether transverse, diagonal or straight.

Just inside the entrance, with its dark wings in which to deposit wreaths, stand four life-size, unidentifiable and almost faceless figures of men, a gruesome and fearful memorial to the twenty-four thousand unknown German soldiers that lie in a great ossuary at their feet. As we leave this awesome place a party of Germans arrive. They nod solemnly to us, as we do to them. We drive away, and I note that it seems a considerable time before Leopold resumes conversation again. It is plain that we are both affected by the heavy funereal atmosphere of the German cemetery. We miss the gay flowers on the graves and the inspiring biblical phrases inscribed on the headstones in British cemeteries.

Further north we reach Vladslo and enter another great German cemetery, similar to that near Langemark and arranged in the same manner. Opposite the entrance, on two blocks of granite, are carved figures of a man and a woman, the work of Kathe Kollwitz, a famous German sculptress and print-maker. The kneeling figures, which are in fact studies of the sculptress and her husband, represent the bereaved mother and father of all the dead buried in the cemetery. The woman's shrunken and bowed figure, and the man's staring eyes of bewilderment, surely cannot fail to stir pity in the hearts of all beholders. The remains of over ninety thousand German soldiers lie in the two cemeteries we see this day.

On our way we pass a striking monument to the memory of Georges Maria Guynemer, 1894–1917, the most famous French fighter pilot of the First World War. This memorial is at Poelcapelle and was erected by Belgian pilots in recognition of his brilliance during the war. In February 1915 Guynemer tried unsuccessfully to join infantry and cavalry regiments, and turned only as a last resort to service in the air. He made his first flight in 1915 and joined *Les Cigognes*—the Storks—as a corporal pilot. He served with the squadron and shot down fifty-three enemy aircraft, but failed to return from a sortie in September 1917.

There are many British cemeteries in this area of the Ypres salient and it would take days to visit them all. We come to Tyne Cot, near Passchendaele, where a great battle was fought in October–November 1917. In the centre of the cemetery is a massive German blockhouse, which the Australians captured against fierce and prolonged resistance. Total British graves here exceed twelve thousand, and the names of thirty-five thousand soldiers with no known graves are carved on many wooden panels. The St Julien Memorial close by commemorates two thousand Canadians, some of whom suffered death in the first gas attack by the Germans in April 1915.

Our next visit is to the 'Pool of Peace', the name given to one of the nineteen craters which resulted from the blasting of huge mines by the British as a preliminary to the battle of Messines Ridge. In 1930 the Reverend Tubby Clayton appealed in *The Times* for the preservation of one of the craters and thus saved it from being filled in. Lord Wakefield responded by purchasing

the one known as 'Lone Tree Crater'. He handed it over to
Talbot House, who named it the 'Pool of Peace'. The ninety-one
thousand pounds of ammonal which were used in its blasting
made a hole forty feet deep and two hundred and fifty feet
across. Leopold and I sit down beside it in the warm sun. It is
shaded by a ring of thick bushes and there is not a single ripple
on the surface of the water. It is indeed a pool of peace.

Two hundred yards away is Lone Tree Cemetery, which is
situated in a meadow and rather too near farm buildings and
cowsheds. One's approach to the entrance of the cemetery is
unavoidably through mire and dung, caused by the cattle who
linger by the cemetery gate, which is within a few feet of a pond
at which they drink. This is a bit awkward, but once through the
gate the cemetery is immaculate and gay with beautiful flowers.
Particularly striking is a lone tree in excellent shape, planted
many years ago. Most of the hundred or more headstones in this
cemetery are for men of the Royal Irish Rifles who were killed on
the day the nineteen mines were blasted.

The village of Messines today is fully restored and Leopold
invites me down into the crypt of the church. He tells me that
according to the local people Hitler often sheltered in this crypt
when he was a lance-corporal in the First World War. In the
1939–45 war he passed the church and told one of his staff about
these events. The information was passed on to the villagers,
and today this legend is regarded by them as historical fact.

My friend is hungry, so we drive to a café. He never eats a mid-
day meal, and contents himself with a bottle of Vittel or Evian
water. It is still early when we finish the meal and he suggests we
go to le Touquet, which is quite close. We visit a Monsieur
Loridan, who is the local Deputy Burgomaster. It is not long
before I realise why I am here. We enter the DB's fine modern
house and Madame Loridan brings bottles of beer into the dining
room. After cordial greetings Madame invites me over to a
particular part of the room, and Leopold then informs me that I
am now standing directly over the front line of the old British
trenches.

As I sip my glass of beer, I am fascinated to reflect that, as a lad
of seventeen, I must have passed many times across this very
ground. I think, too, of my young companion Bill Bailey, shot
through the head at breakfast-time one lovely June morning in

1915. Then there was young Carroll, who, apparently for no reason at all, exposed his head and shoulders above the top of the parapet and paid the ultimate penalty. I reach back in my memory to the images of the two young lads who were, for a brief while, my daily companions. I was only just beginning to know them when they were suddenly snatched away. Yet, here am I well over the allotted span. It baffles me to think about it.

The DB is a jolly, well-set-up man of seventy-three, who no doubt works hard in his transport business. In spacious sheds are three articulated lorries—a further three are out on the road—and three large American estate cars. There is a very long inspection pit excavated in the floor of one of the sheds. When it was dug out several years ago a number of German gas cylinders were discovered. The steel casing of the cylinders is half an inch thick, and they now form substantial mountings for lathes and other machines in the workshop. Leopold keeps up a rapid conversation, delving into the local history with Madame Loridan, who appears to be an authority on the subject, while I sit happily smoking one of the DB's fine Havana cigars as he pours out another bottle of beer. Soon darkness falls and we leave our kind hosts for Poperinge.

*   *   *   *

It is another fine day, and my companion calls for me in good time. He has heard from the War Graves Commission at Ypres and we make for Noeux-les-Mines cemetery, where General Wing's grave is said to be. The information we have been given is correct and we soon find it. I was seventeen when the Battle of Loos was fought, and I remember being quite scared at the general's death. Somehow it didn't seem right to me that a high-ranking officer should be killed. His death made me realise more than anything else that you can be killed in war no matter what your rank is. The inscription on the general's headstone reads: 'O Lord, my helper, and my Redeemer'. I write in the visitors' book, 'I came to see the grave of Major-General F. C. V. Wing, CB, CMG,' and sign my name as a private of the 6th Queen's, 12th Division.

The next place we head for is Souchez, where Leopold says there is a great French cemetery. As we belt along he talks incessantly, and I frequently delve into my store of youthful memories, which have lain almost undisturbed for years during a busy working life but now rush from the distant past and jostle for recognition. I imagine that I am back in the ranks again with my pack on my back, four abreast in column of route, marching. I seem to hear snatches of that old hymn 'Holy, Holy, Holy', and the sound of mouth-organs. I'm amazed at the distances we lads used to march in full kit, for it was seldom we ever got a lift. Did we really march all this way, I ask myself. But we did, and there were not many stragglers either. We must have been fitter than we realised.

On reaching Souchez we climb to high ground and enter the French Military Cemetery of Notre Dame de Lorette. The first thing that strikes me is a huge beacon tower which is always lit at night. Close by is a large and imposing chapel; waiting to enter is a party of men wearing purple silk armlets. They belong to a French ex-servicemen's organisation and act as guardians of the chapel. They acknowledge us as we pass into the chapel, but do not speak. One of them follows us as if to ensure that we observe the utmost decorum as we move around.

This building is clearly meant to be a perpetual memorial to the dead, and is rich in its design and in the materials used in its construction. High up on both arms of the transept are three beautiful stained glass windows given by the British Empire. One part of the chapel is used as a special memorial to thousands of soldiers with no known graves, some of whose remains lie in the ossuary below. The superb richness and elegance of French art and craftsmanship are used to the full, and the effect is almost overpowering.

There are twenty thousand graves in this cemetery, and the remains of a further twenty thousand soldiers lie in seven ossuaries. Outside the chapel, adorning the many rows of crosses erected on the huge expanses of the cemetery, are hundreds of hydrangea shrubs, which are beginning to develop pink blooms. The whole place seems alive with gardeners, and there is a constant sound of machinery in the air.

There are extensive facilities and a large restaurant for the visitors; also a canteen for the staff. Every need seems to be catered for, and the whole set-up is run with the usual French commercial efficiency. Across the valley beyond Souchez, Leopold points out the great Canadian memorial on Vimy

Ridge, the scene of a brilliant attack on 9 April 1917, the day that the battle of Arras commenced. He also mentions that Hitler visited Vimy Ridge on 2 June 1940.

We continue our journey to Cambrai and soon reach Arras, the city that the 12th Division defended against the enemy for months—its mayor describing the division as 'Defenders and Deliverers of Arras'. Leaving the city, we drive along the Cambrai road. We pass Feuchy cemetery and the terrain becomes familiar to me. I tell Leopold that we will soon see the place where the village of Monchy-le-Preux once stood, on the left-hand side of the road. There is no mistaking the low hill that I gazed at many times each day for a period of nearly six months in 1917, except for occasional spells of rest in the villages behind Arras. Instead of a pile of rubble I find a living community, still called Monchy-le-Preux. There it is, neatly wooded on the outskirts; a church spire stands proudly in the centre with houses clustered around.

We drive slowly, looking for a turning to take us to the village, and I realise that we are moving close to the ground that the 8th Cavalry Brigade passed over on 11 April 1917 in their hopeless attempt to assist the 12th and 37th Divisions to storm Monchy's powerful defences. Galloping across a mile or more of open country covered in snow, and in full view of the Germans during the whole length of the charge, they were crushed by a terrible hail of fire from machine guns, artillery and rifles, delivered by an enemy entrenched behind massive barbed-wire defences.

But now all is quiet and peaceful. Except for the occasional motor vehicle swiftly passing along the Cambrai–Arras road, the only noise I hear is the gentle swaying of the corn growing near the roadside. I feel keyed up a bit, for I never thought I'd ever see this village again, where so much happened to me when I was young. When we enter the village at the top of the low hill the first person we see is a middle-aged man carrying a basket of strawberries. Leopold shouts to him and he comes over and stands beside the open window of the car, with the basket in front of him. After some preliminary talk, Leopold informs him that I am an old British soldier who fought on the slopes of Monchy for several months in 1917. On hearing this the good man beams with pleasure, shakes hands with both of us and passes the basket through the car window, inviting us to help ourselves, which we do without a second bidding. From him we learn that German cavalry first entered the village in October 1914 and set fire to it, destroying the church, twenty-four houses and a large barn. Later, fourteen bodies were found in the ashes. I have an idea that this piece of information is not generally known.

Expressing our best wishes and thanks to the friendly Frenchman, we move on. Close to the church I see a magnificent bronze statue of a caribou, with its head raised as if bellowing out a challenge. It stands on top of a concrete German stronghold. On a plaque beneath is the following inscription in English and French:

Newfoundland.

Terre Neuve.

I am so impressed by this fine statue that I am determined to discover the story behind it when I return home.[1]

Near the caribou memorial is the restored village church; standing in front of it is a pathetic group of bereaved women and children carved in stone. It is a memorial to the villagers who lost their lives during the war, and it is pleasing to read the inscription, which indicates that the people of the Isle of Wight gave generously towards the cost of erecting it. There is further evidence of help given by the Isle of Wight. Two stout brick piers support a pair of large iron gates at the entrance to the civilian cemetery. A plaque on one of the piers bears the following inscription:

To the glory of God and in memory of the valiant sons of
France and Britain who together laid down their lives in

---

[1] I later wrote to the Department of Veteran's Affairs, Government of Newfoundland and Labrador. They were most kind and co-operative, and sent me a fine book entitled *The Fighting Newfoundlander* by Colonel G W L Nicholson, a government publication. From this I learnt that there are five Newfoundland battlefield memorial sites. At each of these a massive bronze caribou stands in a natural setting surmounting a rocky crag, from which he surveys the country in the direction in which the Newfoundlanders faced the enemy. There are four in France—at Beaumont Hamel, Gueudecourt, Masnières and Monchy-le-Preux. The fifth is at Courtrai in Belgium. A section in the book headed 'The Men who Saved Monchy' gives a thrilling account of the sheer heroism and guts of a handful of men from the Royal Newfoundland Regiment under Lieutenant-Colonel James Forbes-Robertson who, on 14 April 1917, during the early stages of the battle of Arras, brought a strong German counter-attack to a halt.

The Newfoundland Regimental Memorial at Monchy-le-Preux.
Commonwealth War Graves Commission

*defence of liberty. These gates set up in 1925 are the gift of the
Isle of Wight to Monchy-le-Preux.*

Inside the village church we meet the curé and his sister, from
whom we learn that, towards the end of the fourteenth century,
there lived a St Jean de Monchy-le-Preux, a humble shepherd.
According to a booklet the curé gives us, this saintly shepherd
was gifted with extraordinary powers of healing. He was held in
the highest esteem, especially by Pierre Ranchicourt, Bishop
of Arras from 1463 to 1499. By a decree of 20 October 1625 and
one of 5 July 1634 by Pope Urban VIII, it was stipulated that
where a person had the reputation of having lived a saintly life
before 1534 his name should be added to the canonical list of
saints. Thus, the name Saint Jean Le Berger (shepherd) has
been revered by the villagers of Monchy to this day. His
mausoleum in the church was destroyed during the French
Revolution in 1793, but later on a certain Count Oudard
provided an even more magnificent mausoleum, the marble
structure resting on four supports resembling crouching lions.
Then came the Great War when the entire village was
destroyed. During the building of the present church on the old
site, one of the four lions was discovered, but the bones of the
saintly old shepherd must still lie close to those of many soldiers,
both British and German, who died during the capture of
Monchy in 1917.

On leaving the church we come upon an imposing monument
erected to the memory of the 37th Division. This fine division
fought side by side with the 12th for many months in 1917. The
memorial has a triangular plinth and mounted on it are life-size
figures of three soldiers. The inscription on the memorial
records the names of all the units that served in the division. I
search the surrounding country with binoculars and locate the
village of Roeux about four kilometres north. There was fierce
fighting there in May 1917, at the time I rejoined the 37th
Machine Gun Company after being wounded on the Somme in
October 1916.

I leave this lovely village on the low hill with considerable
happiness and contentment, now that I have seen it fully
restored to a peaceful existence. My visit to Monchy has stirred
up my memory more than anything else on my tour with

Leopold. I felt that I must find out why the people of the Isle of Wight should take such a keen interest in this ill-used little village.[1]

*   *   *   *

Resuming our journey along the Cambrai road, I begin to look on the right for a signpost giving directions to the village of Wancourt, from which the famous Wancourt Line derived its name. Once Monchy and its immediate frontages facing the Germans were finally in our hands, the Wancourt Line became a powerful barrier against any attempt to recapture the battered village. We pass over the approximate position where the Wancourt Line ran across the Cambrai road. I can see the location of Spade Trench opposite the Bois du Sart, where Edwin Short and Jock Hershell were killed. They were staunch warriors, utterly reliable, and their loss had a marked effect on the morale of my gun team.

Leopold wants to see the terrain over which the tanks moved on the right flank of the Cambrai attack, which was covered by the 12th Division. I am eager to see the city for the first time, though, had there been sufficient reserves to back up the performance of the tanks, I might well have entered Cambrai fifty-five years ago.

It is very hot in the Cambrai streets and Leopold suggests ice cream; soon we are sitting comfortably on a seat in the main thoroughfare. I consume three separate dollops of the stuff. If only for a few minutes, I am a youngster once again. I smile as I consider how ridiculous it is, that as a septuagenarian I am actually eating ice cream in Cambrai, in civvies, instead of as a conquering hero in soldier's uniform. Of course, now I am here Cambrai seems just like any other French town, but I'm grateful to be alive to see this city at my time of life.

[1] On my return home I wrote to the Town Clerk of Newport, Isle of Wight. He kindly contacted the Isle of Wight County Press and in due course that newspaper lent me some old cuttings. From these I discovered that Monchy was adopted by the people of the island in the early twenties. A committee was formed under the chairmanship of Major-General J E B Seeley to raise funds. The islanders subscribed enthusiastically and their generosity soon began to take the form of practical assistance. The first bountiful action was the supply in 1924 of sheets to 374 villagers in 146 families. Next came the purchase of land on which to bore wells for water, of which there was a great scarcity. Other good works followed.

We leave for Masnières, where the St Quentin canal coils like a snake. On high ground just outside Masnières the car stops. I realise I am very near the spot, where, at 8 am on 22 November 1917, I was wounded by German machine-gun fire. I want to wander off for a while to see if I can pin-point the exact spot where Jerry got me, but the old battle-ground lies heavy with corn and other crops. I turn away, as it is not reasonable to trample about regardless of any damage I am sure to do. 'Never mind, George,' says Leopold. 'I'll take your photo looking towards the spot,' and so he does. A mile or so further along the road we see the Masnières caribou statue, looking magnificent at the top of a pyramid of huge rocks.

Continuing on the way towards Banteux, I see the village of la Vacquerie, which is close to where my machine gun section commenced moving forward in support of the 6th Queen's at dawn on 20 November 1917, the first day of the Cambrai attack. From a raised piece of ground I am able to survey Vacquerie Valley stretching from left to right in front of me; it continues to the right as far as the ridge above Masnières. Seventy-two tanks allotted to the 12th Division crawled forward along this valley at the rate of fifty yards per minute, but several broke down through engine failure. When Ludendorff counter-attacked ten days later, some of these tanks were captured, taken to Courtrai for repair and used against the Allies later on.

★   ★   ★   ★

We drive on into the Somme area and visit the great memorial at Thiepval, a village captured by the Aussies after terrific fighting in 1916. The memorial is a huge arch-like structure of red brick and can be seen for miles around. I notice that the steps and paving under the arch are covered with fragments of bricks which have fallen from above. It is a pity that such an imposing memorial is not weathering well.

As we approach Albert we glimpse in the distance the gold figures of the Madonna and Child, high up on the basilica tower; it is a thrilling sight after all these years. Standing in the town square at the foot of the great church, I peer through binoculars at the golden summit of the tower. The rich gold leaf, which extends down to the frieze at the bottom of the cupola, seems glorious. So magnified are the figures of the Virgin and Child that I feel I could stretch out a hand and touch the babe's head.

We enter the basilica and are amazed at the decorative excellence of the embellishments, whether of stone or metal, used to glorify the interior of the wonderfully reconstructed building. It is staggering to think that the original church was like this one, before Jerry got to work on it. I am indeed grateful that I have been spared to see Albert and enter its renowned church.

Not far from Albert is Crucifix Corner, a place never to be forgotten by those who took part in the centre of the Somme offensive in 1916, and are still living. In five minutes my good friend speeds me there; I am speechless when I look up and gaze at the crucifix I first saw fifty-six years ago and from which this terrifying area took its name. It is still in the same position, though a fringe of trees and an elongated pile of stone chippings, presumably for road repairs, obscure the mound on which it stands.

The crucifix is on top of a bank, at the point where the road from Albert to the front line forks. With binoculars I scan the cross minutely. The figure of Christ seems newly silvered; in a cavity between the nailed feet I notice a bird's nest. The cross itself looks like cast iron, moulded on the surface like the bark of a tree. I was eighteen when I first passed this cross, and I well remember looking up at His face for a few moments as I was passing on the road to the front line at la Boisselle, and wondering what He really meant to us poor soldiers going into battle where the chances of survival were pretty slim. German logistic experts made no mistake as to the extreme importance of Crucifix Corner to the British, and it was pounded constantly with heavy shells from howitzer batteries, causing pandemonium and destruction among the troops and animals.

Leaving Crucifix Corner, we take the left fork and come to Blighty Valley Cemetery close to Authuille Wood and Aveluy Wood. We walk along the edge of a field where rows of young plants are growing. Leopold bends down and picks up a jagged lump of shrapnel. I follow suit, and we soon realise that the whole field is loaded with metal scrap from German shells which exploded during the Somme offensive. Fragments are sold to visitors at a franc a piece, but the usual method of disposal is through scrap-metal merchants, which practice has been going on for well over fifty-years—there seems no end to the source of supply. I keep one nasty-looking piece as a souvenir.

Blighty Valley Cemetery lies in the centre of this horseshoe-shaped valley, whose wooded slopes rise to where the old British front line ran at the commencement of the Somme battle. On my right I see Aveluy Wood, through which my company struggled with its guns and equipment on the way to the front line at la Boisselle.

The sun is beginning to go down and it is time to return to Belgium. We leave the quietness of the cemetery and walk back to the road. Everything seems so beautiful on this glorious summer's evening, reminding me of similar beautiful evenings in the blazing month of July 1916, when I was in the front line on the other side of Aveluy Wood not far from here. Is it my imagination that nature seems to be so very kind where the cemeteries are?

It is a long way back to Poperinge, and Leopold really tears along. I am starving, having eaten nothing since the ice cream at Cambrai. Madame Lucienne welcomes us with fried eggs and a monster bowl of golden chips. Tomorrow I must ask to meet Leopold at the War Graves Commission in Ypres, to obtain information regarding the location of my step-father's grave.

*   *   *   *

It is another lovely morning. After breakfast I look for Adam in the garden. I talk to him and he puts his head out almost at once. Taking the bus to Ypres, I slowly walk round the Cloth Hall and St Martin's Cathedral, gazing at the stonework and admiring its beauty and perfection. Even after so many years I find that the very name 'Ypres' fills me with a sense of homage and sorrow. That such complete destruction should fail to break the will and spirit of our soldiers who died defending the rubble is almost unbelievable. It is certain that so long as civilisation exists, the name Ypres will remain immortal.

St George's Memorial Church is close at hand and in the library I pore over the pages of the East Surrey Regiment's official history, which contains the following entry relating to my step-father: Serjeant W. J. Humphrey,
9th Batt East Surrey Regiment, age 33,
Died of wounds, Jan 10th, 1916.

At the office of the War Graves Commission I join Leopold, and we are given the information that we need. The staff there are most pleasant and co-operative as they dig out the details from the vast number of registers of the dead. We drive to Lijssenthoek Cemetery near Poperinge and I soon find the grave. I corresponded with my step-father when we were both in the trenches, he in the Ypres salient, and I at Festubert, but our plans to meet each other were not realised. The inscription on his headstone reads:

'Thy will be done.'

Leopold takes my photograph as I stand beside the grave. Nearby I notice a headstone on which is inscribed the words:

Major F. H. Tubbs, VC
7th Battalion Australian Infantry, 20th Sept, 17.
'Our dearly loved son and brother.
Called to higher service.'

We chat with the master-gardener and he shows us round the workshops where the various machines are maintained and overhauled. There is a large nursery near the cemetery where thousands of young plants are reared. It is clear to me that the War Graves Commission, on behalf of the nation, are doing honourable and devoted service in their work of beautifying the burial places of our dead.

Leopold has to leave me for a couple of hours. He drops me at Ploegsteert Wood, beside a sign pointing to four small cemeteries, namely, Mud Corner, Toronto Avenue, Ploegsteert and Rifle House. Before setting off to visit them, I sit down for a rest beside a splendid cornfield, nearly full grown, and look across the field to 'Plugstreet' where many bloody fights were waged during those far-off years. It is early evening, the sun is still well up, and the air is clean and quiet. Seated in this pleasant place, so different from the gruesome and battered appearance it once presented, I allow my thoughts to wander. . . .

I think I must have dozed off for a few minutes. I get up and cross the cornfield by a narrow track. The evening sunshine is brilliant as I approach the broad fringe of Ploegsteert Wood. The trees are not fully grown—but the general impression is of freshness and flourishing vigour. I see nobody about and have the feeling that I'm on a lonely jaunt. This proves to be the case, for during two hours in the wood I meet not a single soul.

The first cemetery is Mud Corner on the edge of the wood. I ponder on the reason for this particular name. The countryside is not hilly, but I notice that the surrounding land slopes slightly towards this point. Here is the answer. I visualise this depression in winter during the war awash with water; sundry troops passing in and out of the wood all hours of the day and night, cursing and blinding as they stagger through the mud carrying loads of rations, ammunition, barbed-wire reels, stores and so on; and stretcher-bearers encumbered with the dead and severely wounded.

I enter the cemetery, which is not a large one but intimate and friendly. The great cemeteries are awesome and almost frightening. I walk along the rows of headstones, so clean and erect. They are mostly Australians who lie here. Poor chaps. What a long way for them to come to fight and die for us in this foreign field. What young and vigorous men they must have been. There is neither register nor visitors' book here—perhaps they are in one of the other cemeteries in the wood. I close the gate quietly behind me.

It is a fifteen-minute walk to the next cemetery along a narrow track that is getting very muddy. A lone bird protests at my intrusion and follows me as I slip about. He is only a few yards off, and now and then I catch a glimpse of him as he flutters through the branches. It is a bit eerie walking alone in this wood with nobody to talk to. Does this bird resent me breaking the quietness here? To give myself some assurance, I start to whistle loudly and shrilly through my teeth as if I'm calling a bus to stop. This silences him for a little while, but soon he challenges me, and I join him in a kind of duet. At last I reach a War Graves Commission signpost which says, 'Toronto Avenue—LEFT, Ploegsteert Wood and Rifle House—RIGHT.' I go left to Toronto Avenue.

This, too, is a neat and friendly resting place for departed warriors, set like a jewel in a small circle of trees. There is nothing to frighten anybody here. Like Mud Corner, the grass is beautifully kept, its edges trimmed to perfection; the headstones are dead in line and pretty summer flowers adorn the weedless soil at their feet. I count the various ranks as inscribed on the headstones: one captain, three sergeants, one corporal, 110 privates. I rest here a while. As I retrace my steps to the signpost, the little bird starts up again, and I follow his trill as he flits alongside.

Sliding and slipping over the mud I reach Ploegsteert Wood Cemetery, which is rather larger than the first two but no less well kept. The gardeners at these cemeteries do not operate in a slipshod fashion. They work faithfully and well. I feel a bit tired as I come to Rifle House. The bronze locker containing the register and visitors' book for the four cemeteries is here and I record my visit. Like the gates of all the British cemeteries, the lockers are never locked. I sit on a seat as the great red sun pours its evening glow on this consecrated place. Not far away a cuckoo sings; it is a heavenly sound. It is my good fortune to have survived the war, but life has not been all beer and skittles. In fact it has often occurred to me that if I had been killed I would have escaped a lot of life's worries. But as I relax in the sunshine it is wonderful to be alive. I've already passed the so-called allotted span, so I have much to be thankful for.

Sitting here alone with my thoughts I feel a deep sympathy for these dear departed men who died so young. I recall how often I myself might have been enrolled in their lifeless ranks, and perhaps lie with them in these quiet and beautiful cemeteries. Of my memories of life in the trenches, the one thing I cherish more than anything else is the comradeship that grew up between us as a result of the way of life we were compelled to

Rifle House Cemetery, Ploegsteert Wood.
Commonwealth War Graves Commission

lead—living together under the open sky, night and day, fair weather or foul, witnessing death or injury, helping in matters of urgency, and above all, facing the enemy. Such situations were the solid foundation on which our comradeship was built. It has been said that such comradeship died when the war ended. The sun is sinking now. I am glad I came here alone and not in a crowd. If I had, I should not feel as I do now. I would not have recaptured my spiritual link with them, the dead soldiers. I think earnestly of the whole futility of war. Politicians would do well to tour all the cemeteries in France and Belgium and resolve never to act rashly, nor deliver ultimatums or threats of any kind, but to hold their hand, striving to their utmost to achieve harmonious relations with all peoples.

It is time for me to leave this hallowed place and return to the road. As I tramp back along the muddy track winding through the wood, I neither see nor hear my feathered friend. Leopold is at the rendezvous and takes me to a little restaurant for supper. It is all over now and I've done what I wanted to do. Though late in life I've experienced a glimmer of youth and heard the voices of my young companions again.

*   *   *   *

I am up like a lark this morning and Leopold drives me to Hazebrouck, where he gives me parting gifts for my wife and daughters. His friendship and untiring efforts to show me round the battlefields amaze me, and I earnestly hope that he has benefited from drawing on my fund of youthful memories.

I am now on the French ferry *Cote D'Azur* bound for Folkestone. Sitting close to me are five Asiatics. They speak in a foreign tongue, but all of them have British passports. With my full whack of duty-free goods, I pass through the Customs via the green channel.

A few days after I returned from Belgium Leopold sent me a cutting from a newspaper, *La Voix Du Nord*, dated 27 June 1972. It described the tragic death of an agricultural worker, aged 34, married with two children, who had been killed by a 170 mm shell of the 1914–18 war, near Ploegsteert Wood. It is a sad case, and seems to bear out the belief that many Tommies accept, 'If it's got your number on it, there is no escape.'

On the Wire by William Roberts, RA, a watercolour inspired by *With a Machine Gun to Cambrai.*   *Reproduced by kind permission of the artist*

Appendix

Some letters received by the author

From Mr James W Autry, Manchester   29 May 1970

You will, no doubt, be surprised to receive
this letter, but I saw in 'The Boy David' the report
of your book 'With a Machine Gun to Cambrai' and I
was fortunate enough to have the loan of this book,
of which, previously, I had no knowledge. I am
trying to obtain a copy from HMSO, as I was very
interested in it.

I am ex-Emma Gee from the 9th and 41st
Divisions. I noted you mentioned we relieved you
on one occasion and your book brought back vivid
memories.

I joined under age in the 1/7th Battalion,
Manchester Territorials, and was just in time for
the mobilisation on 4 August 1914. We proceeded
to the Dardanelles, where, as you know, we had a
devastating time.

Upon arriving back in France they were asking
for volunteers for the Machine Gun Corps and I was
sent to Belton Park, on an NCO course. I
appreciated your remarks about the staff and
instructors there and I think your views were
pretty general, as far as the 'Old Sweats' were
concerned.

Do you remember the RSM? I cannot think of
his name, but I do know everyone on the camp -
officers, NCOs and men - were frightened to death
of him - and yet off-duty he was quite human.

I remember one time I was acting Orderly
Sergeant. As you know, crimes there did not go
on your charge sheet unless they were serious and
the majority of charges were manufactured to give
the officers a chance of conducting the Orderly
Room. In this particular case the lad on charge
was charged with being drunk and AWOL, which was
incorrect. The officer, after the usual
procedure, gave him 28 days' CB and 7 days'
RW. Well, immediately after the verdict, down
came the RSM's stick on the table and he roared,
'You, a junior officer, cannot give a sentence
like that. Discharge the accused with a warning.'
Which was done, but the officer's face was white
and he went sick the following morning.

After training I went on 14 days' leave and
was posted to the 41st Division. During the
Somme attack I was wounded, but not seriously
enough for Blighty, and when A1 again I was posted
to the 9th Division, with whom I remained for
the duration.

We went to Italy when the Ityes were thinking
of packing it in and then back to France for the
big push in March 1918, when Jerry got us on the
run. I remember at Bapaume we had to make a
hurried retreat and my Nos. 1 and 2 on our gun
were killed, so I up with the tripod and yelled
to my No.4 to pick up the gun and we ran for I

should think a couple of miles and found a new
position. I set up the tripod and was waiting for
the gun to arrive when the No.3 arrived with the
spare parts and said, 'I shouted a long way back
that No.4 had been wounded but you didn't hear me.'
I said to him, 'Then why didn't you pick up the gun?'
He said, 'I wasn't told to.' You can imagine what
I said to him.
     There are a few of us around in Manchester and
we get together occasionally and have a natter about
the old days ...
     I daresay you saw the report in the last
issue of 'The Boy David' journal that my wife and
I had just celebrated our Golden Wedding.

From Father P Dominic Devas OFM,* Liverpool   27 February 1970

          I want to let you know how very much indeed
I enjoyed your book. You covered, here and there,
ground once familiar to me and never forgotten,
especially Aveluy Wood, Crucifix Corner, Thiepval,
Ovillers, Contalmaison, Mametz Wood - in a word,
the Somme; and, more peaceful, Allouagne. My
experiences were indeed very different. I am an
RC priest, and - I'm 82 now - was a Chaplain in
the war. I'm afraid your view of Chaplains was -
is? - rather dim, and I'm not surprised: but I
don't think we were all alike. With the 1/6
Gloucesters - 48th Division - and later (the 48th
went to Italy) with the 37th attached to the
S. Lancs, I was not a stranger to the front line,
and knew what the proximity of bullets sounded
like but of course my usual place was with the
MO in the First Aid Post. I had none of the
fierce experiences you write so vividly about.
But the saddest part of your book is at the very
end when you describe in such simple, poignant
language the appalling conditions facing the ex-
soldier in the 1920s. Your book, so neatly
produced, is well worth the modest 6/6 required,
though, I confess, its title 'to Cambrai' led
me to hope it would cover the final attack and
entry in 1918 with which I was very familiar.
I hope fate has been kind to you in your retirement. The countryside of Kent - if that's where
you are - is lovely indeed.

*Author of <u>From Cloister to Camp</u> (London, 1919)

From Mr Alan Brown, Sheffield, Yorkshire   28 March 1971

I have just read your book 'With a Machine Gun
to Cambrai' and I found it very interesting.
Truly a genuine story, so much so I felt I must
write to you stating my appreciation of it.

Like you, I was in that war and still have
vivid memories of it, some good and some not so
good. I joined up at 18 years old on January
1917 - rather later than you - but I still
remember 1 July 1916, the day you were on the
Somme, when the news came through that our local
City Battalion - 12th Bn Yorks and Lancs - were
practically wiped out: a roll call at the end
of that day was about 40 men left out of 700.

I joined up in 1917 at 18 years old - 1/5th
Battalion Duke of Wellington's Regiment - just
the average type, 5'6", elementary school
education. We went to Cramlington, Northumberland,
like a bunch of fluttering chickens but after
three months' intensive training we were like
fighting cocks. Then to France and straight up
to Dickebusch, more north than you were. A bit
rough round Ypres in the 49th Division (the
photograph of the 62nd Division gunners in the book -
that was the reserve Yorkshire Division to ours).
December 1917, went down with gas but at the
casualty clearing station they had to cut off my
boots - trench foot of course. Came to England
and was three months at Beston Hall, Aylesford,
in your lovely county.

Back to Cramlington convalescent. Transferred
to Machine Gun Corps in March - Belton Park,
Grantham - you were there about the same time, I
believe. About a month there and back to France.
To my disgust was sent to 14th Bn MGC, who were
about four miles from where I left the line before,
only our front line then was about five miles away
and this time it was on the Ypres ramparts - not
nice at all. I remained on that salient until the
armistice - a bit rough again but we stuck it out.
Then we came back to Roubaix and fresh reserve
troops went in to Germany. Various jobs with ration
trains to Germany, guarding prisoners, working
parties, ration dumps etc and then came back home
on demob.

I enclose a spare photograph I had, like you,
very youthful-looking. Just an ordinary lance-jack.

My wife and I are quite fit and still enjoy
life, gardening etc - just pensioners but we get
about quite a lot. Derbyshire is on our doorstep
almost. We aren't well off but we get along.
I've never been without a bob in my pocket/all
our married lives and usually a cigarette in my
mouth and a dog by my side.

Forgive me for rambling on so much. Hoping
you and your family are well.

From Mrs Beatrice Buckley, Grimsby, Lincolnshire
23 October 1971

You will not mind my writing, I think. Having read your book, I feel that I want to, very much. Thank you for it.

You had a very tough time so long ago, and you will let me say I have admired you. I am an old woman now (81).

My husband joined the forces early in 1916. He was passed only for home service. But after training in England and Ireland he was sent to France in August 1917. He was 40 years old then. After some time in and out of the trenches, the 1st King's Own Scottish Borderers were sent to the Cambrai area. They met a strong attack, near Masnières, and my husband was killed on 30 November 1917. He has no known grave. He was a private.

You were ill and in risk of your life at that time. I do hope that you now have reasonable health and that the old wound does not cause you trouble.

We had a daughter - now nearly 57, and a son now nearly 55. Their father would have liked to have seen them grow up.

Please excuse me if I have trespassed on your time.

From Mr P Dodson, Maidstone, Kent   16 November 1969

I have read your book 'With a Machine Gun to Cambrai' and being a gunner myself it took me back to France very lifelike. I was with the 2nd Queen's, 22nd Brigade, 7th Division, in the machine gun section when the MGC was formed. My number in the MGC was 19138. Most of the places you mention I have been to, and it gives me the feeling we were very close together during that war.

I find very few of those that experienced that affair are left now - I had two brothers there: one was wounded twice, the other was killed. I myself was very lucky - was never hit once. I find it best to forget about it, unless one does meet a survivor; no one could imagine what it really was like unless they had experienced it. Your book really took me back - the best reading I have found of that war. May we meet some day and I reckon we could give that war a real look-over.

I have just read 'With a Machine Gun to Cambrai'
with more than usual interest. Firstly, as an old
Lewis gunner, in that you were issued with Vickers
at the outset, while we, having learned the Vickers
for more than nine months, were given four Lewis guns
mounted on Vickers tripods before leaving for France.
Then, your seemingly smooth transfer to the newly-
formed Machine Gun Corps intrigues me greatly - when
I recall how our own applications were turned down
flat! Three months or so before the Somme, we
were issued with four more Lewis guns per battalion
and ceased to function as a separate machine gun
section, dumping our Vickers tripods and relying
thereafter on the short-legged folding mountings
attached to the guns. In fact we remained very
much PBI and went 'over the top' with them.

Also, I find that on the evening of 2 October
1916 the 6th Buffs, 12th Division, relieved us
before Gueudecourt, another battalion of our
brigade having passed through what was left of us
(80 out of 550 and no officer) and occupying the
village. We were of the 110th Infantry Brigade,
21st Division, which consisted of the 6th, 7th,
8th and 9th Leicestershires - the 8th Battalion
to be precise. On 25 September we took the Gird
and Gird support trenches and the ground beyond
in front of Gueudecourt, but were held up by a
considerable pocket of 500 or so Bavarians in the
Gird support between us and the Grenadier Guards
on our right. Early the next morning a tank
appeared, and we and the Guards took several
hundred prisoners - following it along the trench
side.

We entrained at Mericourt on the evening of
3 October and detrained at Choques, near Béthune.
Here we received a largish draft, chiefly of
lightly wounded men now recovered from our previous
'excursion' on 14 July when the 110th Brigade took
the wood and village of Bazentin-le-Petit - with
fearful losses.

With company strength of about 90 we marched
up through Vermelles and took over the Hohenzollern
Redoubt sector ('Rum jar land'.). Our front line
(Northampton and Cobden Trenches) ran along the
near side of the Hohenzollern and Potsdam craters.
Supports and reserves were OBs 1, 2, 3, 4, and
Lancashire trench. We held these for 75 days -
front, support, reserve and then back again - until
22 December when we marched - or rather hobbled -
down Barts Alley - through Vermelles - to Sailly-
la-Bourse; thence to your tobacco factory in
Béthune - and then to a blessed Xmas rest at Auchel.

You must have received many congratulations,
but please add mine, and may I venture to hazard
that the title is rather a misnomer, as your

account goes very much deeper than the Cambrai affair. Indeed, you and I seem to have played a sort of 'Box & Cox' unwittingly through several of the war years.

Machine gunners had to use initiative and in sending this I prove the rule. I confirmed your initials first after consulting the requisite phone book and then putting a magnifying glass over your relative's reply from the War Office after he tried to get you demobbed. There I read your initials G W A ... Hence this.

Trust your left leg doesn't bother you too much this cold weather.

From Mr Charles Craske, Folkestone, Kent 19 January 1970

Having just read your book 'With a Machine Gun to Cambrai' you certainly are a pal of mine. .

Enlistment, September 1914, 6th Battalion The Buffs, East Kent Regiment, 37th Brigade, 12th Division - Ace of Spades.

Purfleet - Sandgate - Barossa Barracks. In June, France - Armentieres - Plugstreet - Hooplines. Here I received a bad wound, right thigh. This was a Blighty. After five months I rejoined the 6th Buffs at the beginning of March 1916 in the craters. Oh those Minnies and sleeping out in the waterlogged trenches! Then Arras - Monchy - then the Somme, then Cambrai; when they counter-attacked I was taken prisoner.

I must add after leaving Hohenzollern Redoubt and the craters in April I joined a Stokes mortar battery, 37th Brigade. So I went to Cambrai with a Stokes mortar. I was with yourself all that time really; I must have passed you heaps of times. Yes, I received a blue linen card - Lillers - Crucifix Corner - Ovillers - you with myself know them all.

Your book is a parallel of my life, in fact my biography.

You are to be envied with two lovely daughters. I had no family and my wife died ten years ago. At 79 I am keeping fit and a five-mile walk is nothing. My greatest joy is growing dahlias.

I have just read your book 'With a Machine Gun to Cambrai' and I must congratulate you on a most marvellous effort. To me it was probably the most nostalgic book I have ever read as it almost exactly mirrors my own life during the First World War.

I too was born in 1898 and joined the army, like you, very much under age, in 1914. I found myself in the Royal Field Artillery, was sent to Scotland for training and eventually finished up in North Camp, Aldershot, from where I entrained for France as a member of the Divisional Ammunition Column in the 12th Division. Then through Le Havre and St Omer to stop at Steenwerck. After Armentières, Ploegsteert and all the old familiar places I was transferred to a trench mortar battery early in September 1915 and after a short training period set off for the Loos front; like you I saw a great deal of the action there from a grandstand position.

I then moved with the division through all the places you write about, serving all the time with medium (toffee apples) and heavy (flying pigs) trench mortar batteries (V/12 and X/12 TMB). I managed to get wounded twice, both relatively minor and unluckily neither was a 'blighty one'. I also like you managed to collect a 'Soup Ticket' and an MM. I was one of the lucky ones because after a wounding I always managed to get back to my own unit in the 12th Division.

I remained with the 12th division until it was disbanded in, I think, May 1919. Thus I served in the division throughout its life.

Although we served through some pretty rough ordeals one cannot help looking back with a great deal of nostalgia and remembering primarily the good things. You and I must be among only very few left of the original members of the old division. I only know of one other.

You will, I am sure, be interested in this little anecdote:

The division went back to the Armentières front early in 1918 and the trench mortars were billeted in a small farm at Erquinghem/Lys about 2½ kilometres from Armentières. I became friends with the family that owned it and have kept in touch with them ever since. My wife and I still occasionally visit them and they sometimes come over to stay with us - we are now meeting and entertaining the grandchildren and great-grandchildren of the original owners. To go over to see the family is still one of the grandest treats we get. We usually visit many members of the family, which is spread out among many of the old familiar places which you and I once knew so well.

After the war I came out of the army with no
skills or useful training of any kind so, following
my father's footsteps, I joined the London Fire
Brigade. In course of time this proved a blessing
as I was able to climb the ladder of promotion and
eventually retired as Chief of Fire Staff of the
National Fire Service. So I have been very lucky
in life, which I often find surprising when I think
back to the sort of life we led as youths in the
war.

I have really enjoyed reviving memories in
writing to you of those days of so long ago. It
is, of course, mainly the good things one remembers
most and this is just as well.

Time is marching on for us both, but I do
wish you well and hope you have many pleasant
years ahead.

From Mr A Bunting (late Middlesex Regiment), Chippenham, Wiltshire   4 January 1970

I have just completed the reading of your
experiences during the 1914-18 war and would like to
tell you that I have found your account most
interesting. Although I was fortunate in being
sent to one of the 'jammy' fronts with a Lewis gun
on a mule (ie Mespot) I lost several of my boyhood
friends in France and of course the army of 1914-18
was more or less the same in its loves, hates and
vocabulary.

Like yourself, I did my early training at
Purfleet Camp, where I saw many drafts leave for
France in 1916, and was invalided home to
Liverpool where I enjoyed much hospitality -
also many trips on the 'Iris' and 'Daffodil' across
the Mersey to Birkenhead. Many pleasant memories
as well as the other sort.

As you say, the last survivors of the 1914-18
war will soon have faded away - we have certainly
faded from the memories of those who promised so
much and gave so little. Moreover, any schoolchild
knows about 1066 but is hazy if not ignorant about
the Somme and Gallipoli.

Nevertheless, like yourself, I would not have
missed it - Hooray! Hooray! You will realise from
the foregoing that I am not much of a pen man. I
close by sending you my very best wishes for 1970
and after.

From Mr J W F Skelton, Sydney, Australia   27 November 1972

After all these years I have just read about
your war experiences in the 12th Division. You came
from Croydon. My father was the landlord of the
Fountain Head Hotel in Parchmore Road, Thornton
Heath. It had a bowling green and skittle alley.
We both enlisted on 27 August 1914. I joined the
7th Battalion, Norfolk Regiment, 'D' Company,
13 Platoon in the 35th Brigade. I was in every
action up to March 1918 ...

Your book recalled many sad, also pleasant
memories. Hulluch-Vermelles was nasty; on
13 October 1915 we lost a lot of men, the same at
Flers, Bayonet Trench, October 1916. After you
were badly wounded in 1917 on the Cambrai front
we occupied the German trenches and their very
comfortable dugouts for some days. Everything was
quiet, then one morning (misty) Jerry came over
without any barrage and caught us napping. Our HQ
staff were all killed in their dugouts. Dr
Matheson from Toronto, Canada, threw his badges
away and organised the remnants of our regiment,
thereby stopping the right flank of the German
advance. Our general (35th Brigade) escaped in
his pyjamas. The 29th Division near us lost their
guns. Captain Matheson was later wounded in this
action by aerial machine-gun fire. He died months
later, a very brave gentleman liked by all. We
then went down to Merville and Givenchy, spending
Xmas billeted in that town.

The next big do was when we were suddenly
awakened and transported by motor bus up to Albert
where absolute confusion reigned. Nobody
appeared to know where Jerry was. Our horse
artillery would gallop up in front of us, fire
for a while, then gallop back. Then we would
retire under heavy shrapnel from one ridge down
the valley and up to the next ridge - all very
exhausting. I was wounded and captured and
wounded again by our own airmen at Mons railway
station. There were no Red Cross on our train
though it was full of wounded Tommies.

In 1928 and 1962 on a tour of Europe I
visited the line Arras to Albert. How well I
remember the Grande Place with the deep cellars;
we went through the tunnels and sewers up to the
support line in front of Arras railway station
and advanced to Tilloy Wood and eventually to
Monchy-le-Preux where I saw the cavalry cut up.
Their general, Bulkeley-Johnson - I think that
was his name - was killed in the charge. How
the dead horses smelt as you stood to at dawn!

Well, on Anzac Day, 25 April, we have an annual
march through the city and a service in our Hyde
Park. The Governor of New South Wales, a VC, leads
the march. Many cars carry the old and crippled

ex-servicemen (Boer War veterans), then the
British follow: we used to have 800 men, now we
number thirty. Then follow about 40,000 men with
banners denoting their units. There are over 40
bands in this march. It is a public holiday in
Australia. God willing, I hope to march again
next April... After the service we have a picnic
lunch in our Botanical Gardens overlooking the
harbour with our families and grandchildren.

From Mr F J Heylin, London N7   31 July 1969

Congratulations on your book, which I read ref.
'With a Machine Gun to Cambrai'. As a soldier
serving with the 16th Rifle Brigade, 39th Division,
may I say with oath that everything you published
in your book is absolutely true, and it is the
finest book that I have read and is true to the core.
May I say that when I was reading it a lump came in
my throat. I was at the age of 17 years in the
trenches at Laventie, just in front of Sailly. We
were in for instruction with the 8th Division, 2nd
Battalion Rifle Brigade. My division must have
followed your division around.
You mention the islands of Festubert, Vermelles,
Hulluch, Givenchy, La Bassée - received a wound
whilst with the bombers in the saps. Also you
mention Cuinchy, another hot spot. I can well
remember the minnenwerfers and whizz-bangs in the
above named places. Also I must say it is true
that every time we came out of the line we were
lined up to read Part Two orders, which stated
that 'the sentence was duly carried out' on many
a Tommy. Well, that is war.
You also mention the tobacco factory at
Béthune - we were billeted there when we came out
of the line. My age now is 71, I am 72 on 25 May
1970. I can remember that when we were at Givenchy
about June 1916 there were plenty of Jocks lying
out in front of our barbed wire and some still
lying on it. When we were sent out at night to
mend the wire we had to crawl through them - it
was awful. You also mention the Hohenzollern
Redoubt, another warm spot, where there was, as you
say, no let-up day or night. May I also say that
your book revived memories for me, also some sad
ones. But never mind, my friend, as an old proverb
says, 'Old soldiers never die, they simply fade
away.'
God bless you, sir.

I have just read and enjoyed your book 'With a
Machine Gun to Cambrai'. When we look back on
World War I tactics compared with modern warfare it
was a murderous business in all the mud and slush of
the Western Front. You chaps certainly had a hell
of a time in France and it is a wonder any one of
you survived at all. I spent my 21st birthday in
the desert in Egypt and wondered if I would be
spared to have my 22nd; but I was, and have had
51 more since. We did not have the hand-to-hand
fighting that you chaps had but there were times
when I wished I were somewhere else. Your pay was
poor. We got 5/- per day, but only 2/- on service
and 3/- deferred till discharge. We could keep
our greatcoats or hand them in and get £5 towards
a suit. Our war was a war to end wars but there
have been wars ever since and things look worse now
than at any time; but you and I will not be taking
part again.

Like you, I was a volunteer and the only thing
we got out of it I think was our lifelong friends,
our comrades in arms (not ladies' arms either). One
of our lads said to me one day, 'I've got these Huns
beat, Fieldie. They can't invent anything that I'm
not frightened of'.

My wife and I retired in 1964. We were
farming our old people's property at Port Levy on
Banks Peninsular of 753 acres, one ram, about 800
ewes plus 300 hoggets and up to 100 cattle, purely
grazing and fattening. We had a house built at
Diamond Harbour, which is in Lyttleton Harbour, and
we can see all the shipping coming and going.

We had our fifteenth annual reunion on 5
November 1969 and there were about 65 present.
We used to get upwards of 150, so the old boys are
thinning out. Our old boys had a reunion in
Auckland a few years back. Two of them were going
down the street and one said, 'You remember the
dope they used to put in our tea to keep us in at
nights? Well, it is just starting to take effect
on me now.'

Well, I hope you and your wife and family
are all well and able to sit up and take a little
nourishment to keep body and soul together. I
felt I must drop you a line or two from way down
under just to express my congratulations on your
good book of true warfare well expressed. Pray
to God we don't have any more wars. I think they
should concentrate on Peace on Earth and not worry
about flying to the moon.

From Mr H Howlett, London SW17   29 September 1969

Firstly let me congratulate you on your book and introduce myself. I was in the original 6th Battalion Queen's and in B Company, also in the Machine Gun Section, and I was amazed when I read of the coal-box episode of Snowy and the two men buried in the deep dugout. I happened to be one of the two that were rescued and from then on I have never contacted anyone from the 6th Battalion. I recognised your photo as soon as I saw it and shall try to find one of mine and will send it on to you.

Well, over 50 years have elapsed since then and it has been a great pleasure writing to you. I am 72 this December - about your age - in reasonably good health and I am hoping you are the same.

From Mr Charles Miles, Welwyn Garden City, Hertfordshire 14 February 1970

Having just finished reading your book 'With a Machine Gun to Cambrai' I feel compelled to write and thank you. I have enjoyed every word of it. I am 76 years of age and served in the Royal Fusiliers in the First World War and with the King's Royal Rifle Corps in the Second World War. In some unaccountable fashion I was enlisted into the 18th (Public Schools)Battalion, Royal Fusiliers. I possess no education whatsoever, having been taught in a County Council school in Stepney in the East End of London. Why I was accepted into this particular battalion was, and has remained, a mystery.

I arrived in France on Sunday 13 November 1915, disembarking at Boulogne and marching up the long hill to St Martin's Camp at the summit. Entraining two days later at Pont de Briques, the battalion arrived at Thiennes, where we detrained. Three days later we marched in stages to Béthune and were billeted in the tobacco factory on the La Bassée road. From here we marched via Beuvry and Annequin to Cambrai, and so up Robertson's Alley and Wilson's Way to the front line for instruction by the King's Own Liverpool Regiment. You will gather from this explanation the immense pleasure I received from reading your book.

From Mr C A Sharman, Tasmania, Australia   22 January 1973

I am writing to tell you how much I enjoyed
reading your book ...
It is a coincidence that on enlistment I was
allotted to 13 Platoon, 'D' Company (26th Battalion,
AIF) later transferred to the machine gun section,
and, after Gallipoli, served·in France with the 7th
Australian Machine Gun Company (Vickers guns).
I found the account of your service in France
extremely interesting and many place names
mentioned brought back memories. It is from such
accounts of the experiences of the man who served
in the ranks that we get the true history of war.